PARIS

COLLECTION *Partance*

PARIS

PATRICE DE MONCAN /J-C.PINHEIRA

Hermé

To my friends "outside the walls"

Willy Andersen,
Satie and Vladimir Spivakov,
Geoff and Shady Calver,
Karl Rickenbacher.

P. de M.

Now as you walk through Paris, alone in the midst of crowds,
Heards of bellowing busses pass you by.

Guillaume Apollinaire

"Each wanderer wherever he strolls, manages to kick up the dust of the past", wrote Henri Calet, one of those numerous Parisian columnists of the nineteenth century who hiked the length and width of the city looking for nourishment to fuel their writings. The dust that these wayfarers trample upon in the streets speaks of the city, of its history and of its daily life. There you will uncover a mixture comprising the ambition of rulers, the dreams of poets, joys and pain, glory and destitution. The smell is royal incense soaked in the blood of numerous revolutions.

Only those willing to walk know how to see Paris. Not only the capital city of Paris, but also the villages of Paris. Paris along the Seine, Paris cafés, Paris gardens, Paris with its beautiful districts and popular Paris, Paris festivals as well as indigent Paris. It is a kaleidoscope bursting with uniqueness and multiplicity.

It was here more than two thousand years ago that Paris began its history one day at a time. Streets, squares, churches, museums, gardens, and hotels and buildings were built, or disappeared or served as a living witness in a vibrant city – not a dead city, or a living museum, but an enduring city of the past, present, and future.

In the Arenas of Lutèce the faraway noise of Gallo-Roman games still roars in the alleys and narrow streets of the Montagne Sainte-Geneviève. The prayers of the Patron Saint of Paris still echo before barbarians on the run. In the towers of Notre-Dame shadows of medieval mysteries hover. In the Louvre, the superb Renaissance façades of the Square Court choke back whispers of schemings and the odor of poison, on the Champs-Élysées the cheers of the Liberation still resound.

Paris is a fantastic puzzle made of stones, of dreams and of disappointments. Its monuments are mirrors of time, symbolic mirrors of the centuries which have made history. The city also mirrors those who have lived here. What would Paris be without Villon, without Nerval, without Balzac, without Verlaine? What would it be without the revolutionary libertines of the Palais-Royal, without the martyr Louis XVI, without the deaths on the barricades, without Général de Gaulle descending the Champs-Élysées? What would Paris be without its foreigners? Without Picasso, without Nijinsky, without Stravinsky, without Fitzgerald, would Paris be the same movable feast described by Hemingway? Few cities have had such a concentration of artists or have had so much influence on universal thought.

"Whoever you may be, here is your master", wrote Victor Hugo in *Paris Guide*.

The small Celtic tribe of the Parisii settled into the Ile de la Cité in the IIIrd century B.C. and founded what would become the Gallic city of Lutèce. Two hundred years later, under the influence of the Romans, this city overflowed the confines of the island and spread onto the left bank of the Seine, essentially on the hill that today is called the Montagne Sainte-Geneviève. The Arenas of Lutèce, the thermal baths of Cluny are living vestiges of this era. The right bank was nothing but marshes. The arenas, situated near the Rue Monge could accommodate up to 17,000 spectators. Gladiator bouts, naval jousts, wild animal combats and theatrical productions all took place there. On a commemorative plaque in the arena can be read this citation by Jean Paulhan: "Passer-by, dream before this first monument of Paris, that this city of the past is also the city of the future and the one of your hopes." Today, there reigns a misleading quietness when one imagines what must have been the clamour of the thousands of "Lutéciens" who came to share the cruel pleasures of the games. Nowadays only a few strollers and students from neighboring schools come here. They come to smoke a cigarette or with their girlfriends to steal a kiss or two.

The Cluny thermal baths represent the most beautiful Gallo-Roman vestige that can be seen in Paris. They date from the end of the IInd century. It is perhaps the last monument constructed by this Gallo-Roman civilization before Lutèce was destroyed by the barbarians in the course of the IIIrd century. In this building which was frequented by the rich boatmen of the city, one finds the "frigidarium" with its two-meter thick walls which have a height of eleven meters. In the lapidary museum are exposed the discoveries made during escavations of the city. Here you can admire the pillar of the Nautes, the oldest known sculpture of Paris. In 1334, the abbot of Cluny acquired these ruins and erected a building which would be reconstructed in 1485 by Jacques Amboise. It is one of the most striking examples of flamboyant Middle Age private architecture. In 1833, Alexandre du Sommarard became its owner and installed a fabulous collection of Middle Age art objects. Eleven years later the state purchased this building and transformed it into a museum. A masterpiece in six panels, the splendid medieval tapestry from the end of the XVth century, the famous *Lady and the Unicorn* is one of its most beautiful treasures.

The Île de la Cité

The Île de la Cité is certainly the district of Paris which has suffered the most from Haussmann's transformation which took place during the middle of the XIXth century. This island which counted more than a thousand small streets in the

XVIIth century, hardly has more than twenty today, and resembles nothing of its former state only a hundred and fifty years ago. Only Notre-Dame, the Conciergerie and the Sainte-Chapelle as well as several rare alleys around the Rue des Ursins, escaped the course of this sort of urban genocide. The Place Dauphine which was closed in before, was deprived of one of its sides in order to make a space which opens onto the façades of the Palace of Justice. The original façades, the small restaurants and the art galleries make this square a good place to day dream. "Every time I am there, I have to plead with myself to cast off a sort of very soft embrace which all too pleasantly keeps me there", writes Breton in *Nadja*. The entire island was re-designed in right angles between 1852 and 1870. Thus in the name of health and public hygiene, some nine hundred interlocking alleys, built little by little, over the course of twenty centuries disappeared. Twenty-five thousand persons were moved, twenty churches collapsed under the strokes of the "builders" shovels. It is true that in the XIXth century this district of Ursins had become a vivacious home for cholera. The narrowness of the alleys, the closeness and the decrepitude of the buildings made this island one of the most unsanitary districts of Paris. It was without air, without light and without water!

Up to a thousand persons a day died during the epidemic of 1832! Certainly urgent measures of hygiene were necessary, but was it necessary to destroy so much? To get a clear idea of this labyrinth of streets which swarmed around Notre- Dame in the middle of the XIXth century, it is necessary to re-read the novel of Eugène Sue: *The Mysteries of Paris*.

It was the bishop of Paris, Monseigneur de Sully who in 1163 decided on the construction of Notre-Dame, on the site of two older churches which were no more than a pile of ruins. It was necessary to wait until 1245 to see it finally accomplished and emerge above this maze of streets. As a cathedral, it was not only a place of prayer. The square in front of the cathedral, much smaller than it is today, was the theater for various spectacles, religious or pagan, such as the Madmen's Folies. The crude humor of this show, far from shocking the crowd, was the very reason for its success. Inside rich and poor could discuss and the sick and homeless could take refuge. In 1430 Henri IV converted to Catholicism there and Louis XIV celebrated his marriage there in 1630. The decoration we see today is not, unfortunately, the original. After the French Revolution, groups of extreme republicans (the Sans-Culottes) vandalized its statuary and its ornamentation. Notre-Dame was no more than an empty and disabled shell when they finished. Viollet-le-Duc was responsable for its renovation, which he carried out between 1845 and 1864. Inspired by the fanciful spirit that made up the romanticism of the Middle Ages and the Gothic era, he added, entrenched, following his own imagination and with total contempt for all historic truth. His work provoked this bitter remark from Prosper Mérimée: "the repairers are perhaps as dangerous as the destroyers."

To gain access to the Sainte-Chapelle, it is necessary to cross the courtyards of the Palace of Justice in which it was enclosed in the XIXth century. Constructed on orders of King Louis IX (Saint Louis) to house the relics of the Passion of Christ, it was part of the former Royal Palace, which it towered above with all its slender grace. When in 1630, this palace was destroyed by a fire, the Sainte-Chapelle was fortunately spared. After the fire, it dominated no more than a small peaceful square surrounded by houses occupied mostly by canons and a few chaplins. Its high colorful stained-glass windows in-

10

spired the admiration of Parisians as much for the historic tales told by their composition as for their rare and changing hues of color. It was said of a new wine, when searching for words to praise its sparkle, that it "was the color of the windows of the Sainte-Chapelle". For a long time it was a favorite meeting place for many Parisians. It was used for grandiose ceremonies and organ concerts.

Facing the Seine, the façade of the Conciergerie, flanked by its towers, evokes Paris of the Middle Ages once again, in spite of additions made to it over the course of the past century.
Constructed at the beginning of the XIVth century, the Conciergerie was not a palace for the kings of France very long. Joinville described it as "the most beautiful sight in all of France". Charles V left it in 1358 in order to settle in the Marais, and no king ever resided there after that. It was then that a part of the palace was transformed into a prison, and that the Grande-Chambre, which had made up part of Louis IX's residence, was used as a courtroom for the major trials of the kingdom. One of these trials was that of Ravaillac, the assassin of Henri IV. It was again in this same Grande-Chambre that the Revolutionary Tribunal was set up in 1793. It was called at that time the Liberty-Room. Except for Louis XVI's trial, all the important trials of the Revolution took place there: those of Marie-Antoinette, Charlotte Corday, Philippe Equality, and Danton, etc. On the ground floor, a part of the Guard Room was, during this period, arranged in prison cells which formed a passageway that was called "Rue de Paris" (Paris Street). The convicts were heaped in these cells to wait for their final trip – that which led toward the guillotine. Between January, 1793, and July, 1794, there were nearly two thousand five hundred of them. Shadows still hover there, whether those of victims or executioners: the Queen Marie-Antoinette, Charlotte Cor-

day, Camille Desmoulins, the poet André Chénier, Robespierre and Saint-Just, etc.

Between the tip of the island, called "la pointe du Vert-Galant", and the Place Dauphine, the Pont-Neuf joins the Île de la Cité to the two banks of the Seine. Constructed from 1578 to 1604, it is the oldest bridge in Paris. A statue of King Henri IV, brought from Florence and offered by Cosme II de Médicis, was placed on the bridge in 1614, four years after his assassination. It was to be pulled down by extreme republican mobs in 1792. The statue we see today is the work of Jean Lescot. It was financed by a national contribution, and its bronze comes from statuaries of Napoléon which were standing in the Place Vendôme and in Boulogne. One of the smelters who was a fervid bonapartist, slipped a statuette of Napoléon, wrapped in political pamphlets, into the right arm of Henri IV. In the base of the statue was placed *The Henriade* of Voltaire. The level of the Pointe du Vert-Galant, just below the Pont-Neuf, is the level of the Île de la Cité when its first occupants lived there. The little garden now on the tip of the island has become a favorite place for fishermen, strollers and a few tramps of Paris. When the July sun beats down on its embankments, many Parisians come to tan while others prefer to sit on a bench and rest in the soft shade of its trees.

It is easy to get to the Île Saint-Louis on foot, by taking the little bridge Saint-Louis, situated behind Notre-Dame. Spanning the two islands, this bridge is, in a way, a sort of abridgment of the history of Paris. There is first, in the very shadow of Notre- Dame, the district of the Ursins, which regroups the authentic Middle Age alleys of the City, then just opposite is the Hôtel de Ville and its square – the former "place des Grèves" - which is now the "place de l'Hôtel de Ville" where for over a thousand years, ceremonies, revolutions

cont. p. 45 ▶

Captions for photographs 1 to 29

1. The *cathedrale* of Paris: Notre-Dame. Built from 1163 to 1345, it was renovated during the XIXth century by Viollet-le-Duc.

2. Notre-Dame. The western rose window with the Virgin and Holy Child in the center, surrounded by the twelve prophets. Above the doors, standing in a row under the trefoil arcades are the twenty-eight kings of Juda and Israel. These are copies dating from 1854. The originals were destroyed by revolutionaries during the French Revolution. They believed them to be the kings of France.

3. The bookstalls facing Notre-Dame along the quai de Montebello.

4. The steeple of Notre-Dame, directly above the crossing of the transept and the nave. The cathedral steeple, destroyed in the XVIIIth century, was rebuilt under the Second Empire. It is 96 meters high. Under its lead covering is a wooden framework.

5. The two towers of Notre-Dame were never finished and have no steeples. In the southern tower is the great bell. It is said that under Louis XIV it was re-cast from women's jewellery. It weighs thirteen tons.

6. A panorama from the northern end of the Ile de la Cité.

7. The golden gates of the Palais de Justice and the Sainte-Chapelle.

8. The Sainte-Chapelle. Built in 1246 on orders from the King of France, Saint Louis (Louis IX). Its stained glass windows date from the XIIIth century. It was partly renovated in the XIXth century,

9. The bridge Pont au Change and the Conciergerie.

10. The bridge Pont-Neuf, the Palais de Justice and the Conciergerie.

11. Summer on the banks of the Vert-Galant park... and sunning on the banks of the Seine.

12. A painter on the bridge Pont des Arts. This bridge, where artists like to show their works, was the first in Paris to be built of metal and wrought iron resting on stone pillars. It was built in 1791, it linked the Louvre and the French Institute.

13. The statue of King Henry IV on the Pont-Neuf, facing the Place Dauphine, dates from 1818.

14. At the end onf the Pont des Arts, the coupole of the French Institute. Under this dome are the Immortals of the French Academy. In Paris, Art can lead to Immortality!

15. The Seine, the Pont des Arts, the Vert-Galant park, the Pont-Neuf and the Ile de la Cité.

16. The church of the Sorbonne. In 1293, Robert de Sorbon created a college of theology which the students baptized the Sorbonne. The college was enlarged in the XVIIth century by Richelieu who had this church built (1628).

17. The Panthéon. Built by the architect Soufflot from 1755 to 1780, the Panthéon was first a church dedicated to the Patron Saint of Paris, Sainte Geneviève. Under the French Revolution it became the tomb for Great Men of the Country. Inside rest Voltaire, Rousseau, Victor Hugo, Zola...

18. The church of Saint-Etienne-du-Mont (on the Place du Panthéon). Built in 1220, enlarged in 1292 and finished in 1620, its decor traces four centures of architectural styles. Racine and Pascal are buried inside.

19. The Hôtel de Cluny. Built in 1485, by Jacques Amboise, it is one of the most beautiful Parisian examples of flamboyant mediaeval architecture.

20. The Luxembourg Palace, from the garden side. Built at the beginning of the XVIIth century by Salomon de Brosse for Marie de Médicis.

21. Sunshine and relaxation in the Luxembourg gardens.

22. Shadows and light on a statue in the gardens.

23. The Panthéon, viewed from a lane in the Luxembourg gardens.

24. The Médicis fountain in the Luxembourg gardens. The jealous Cyclops is ready to crush the shepheard Acis, who is in love with the sea nymphe Galatée.

25. The Saint-Michel foutain (by Davioud, 1860). Located at the beginning of the Boulevard Saint-Michel. In the nitch Saint-Michel, standing on a rock slays the dragon. Above the four marble columns are statues representing Prudence, Strength, Justice and Temperance.

26. Rue de la Harpe. One of the small pedestrian streets near the Boulevard Saint-Michel.

27. The belfry of the church Saint-Germain-des-Prés, which dates from the year one thousand, overlooks the terrace of the Café Deux Magots, one of the seats of existentialism.

28. The Café de Flore, founded towards the end of the Second Empire, has memories of Apollinaire, Picasso, Sartre and Camus.

29. The street market in the Rue de Bucci, in the heart of Saint-Germain-des-Prés.

◀1   2

3

4

5

11

13

21

22

23

26

27

and Parisian dramas have taken place. On the right, the Île Saint-Louis, with its superb town houses and estates and some of the most beautiful embankments of the capital. Behind the island, the Paris of today: the towers of Bercy on the right bank, the Institut of the Arabian World on the left bank – and the Paris of tomorrow, the towers of the Great Library (Grande Bibliothèque) which stand tall announcing the next century.

The Île Saint-Louis

Until the XVIIth century, just east of the Cité, there were two small islands full of willow and popular trees: the Île aux Vaches and the Île Notre-Dame. In 1614, a famous bridge builder named Marie (a bridge on the Île Saint-Louis bears his name) acquired the right, from Louis XIII, to connect the two islands and to build on them. He also had the right to levy a tax on each house for the following 60 years. Corneille writes of his admiration for this new island in le Menteur. He said:
An entire city, built in splendor, Emerged as if by a miracle.
The architect Le Vau was given the mission to construct most of the houses for the aristocrats who wanted to live on the island. The exceptional view of the Seine and Paris which the island offered explains the infatuation of the aristocrats and the rich bourgeois the period had for this new city. The island's success never seems to abate. The most beautiful residence on the Île Saint-Louis is without a doubt the "hôtel Lambert", whose owner is the Baron Guy de Rothschild. A multitude of plaques on the façades of buildings evoke the names of former residents. The names of Racine, Jean-Jacques Rousseau, Apollinaire, Francis Carco or even Le Vau are attached to these illustrious walls. The "hôtel de Lauzun" on the quay d'Anjou was once the home of the painter caricaturist Daumier. He resided here during the last century. The façade is auster, but "gold is in profusion", wrote Daumier. It was on the third floor of this building that Charles Baudelaire, author of Fleurs du Mal lived from 1843 to 1845. Théophile Gautier, with whom he shared "artificially induced pleasures", was his neighbour. At number 15, quay d'Anjou there is a plaque with the name of Cézanne. Other plaques, though less historical, are no less interesting. Thus at number 1, quay de Bourbon, we learn that the daughter of the owner as well as her entire family were sent to the scaffold: the shameless girl had attempted to murder Robespierre, and had failed!

La Montagne Sainte-Geneviève

Facing the Arenas of Lutèce stands the Montagne Sainte-Geneviève, dominated by the dome of the Panthéon. This hill owes its name to the Patron Saint of Paris, Sainte Geneviève. Legend has it that her prayers and her courage prevented the Huns from invading Lutèce in 451. On the slopes of this "mountain" she founded the first convent for women of the city. Upon her death, Clotilde had her buried in the underground chapel of Saint Peter and Saint Paul's, a new basilica constructed by Clovis on the top of Mount Lucoticius. Thus the Abbey Sainte-Geneviève came into existence on the mountain of the same name. It is on this very spot that the Panthéon would be built thirteen centuries later.
Past the Rue Monge there are several steps to climb which lead to the Rue Rollin, a pretty pedestrian street nestled between some rather deformed buildings which a school construction project is busy destroying. At the end of the Rue Cardinal Lemoine stands the house where Ernest Hemingway lived and which he described so well in his famous book about Paris, "A Movable Feast". The Place Contrescarpe comes next and then fur-

ther on the Rue Mouffetard, one of the oldest streets in Paris. Unfortunately restaurants of every nationality and souvenir shops succumbed to its charms and have settled in. The Rue du Pot de Fer, the Rue Lhomond and the Rue de l'Estrapade all lead back to the Panthéon.

It was under the Constituent, in 1791, that this sentence was inscribed on the front of the Panthéon: *To our great men, your country is thankful*. The original purpose of this monument was religious in nature. In 1755, King Louis XV charged the architect Soufflot to build a church in honor of the Patron Saint of Paris on top of the Montagne Sainte-Geneviève. The king had made a vow eleven years earlier to build this structure after recovering from a serious illness. It was twenty years after the formulation of his vow that Louis XV came to place the first stone on September 6, 1764. As this church was only completed at the beginning of the French Revolution, from 1791 the church became the place destined to receive "the ashes of great men from the era of French Liberty". Among the men of the former regime, only Voltaire and Rousseau were judged worthy of "panthéonisation". The others were not considered worthy of their country's recognition. The Panthéon was first of all to serve the cult of "martyrs for Liberty".

The lower windows which punctuated every side of the building were then obstructed to make the structure look less like a church. An engraving of the period illustrating the transfer of Voltaire's remains to the Panthéon, on July 11, 1791, shows all the pomp that the revolutionaries deployed at their high point. It was an attempt to rival religious festivals. There was a veritable republican sanctification of this temple dedicated to citizenship.

In 1806, Napoléon I gave the monument back to the church. However, after the Revolution of July, 1830, Louis-Philippe transformed the Church Sainte-Geneviève into the Panthéon once again. In 1851, Napoléon III made it a church once again. It was only on the occasion of Victor Hugo's funeral (1885) that the Panthéon definitely became the final resting place of the Republic's great men. The interior of the Panthéon is as gigantic as it is cold... The mural decorations are the works of painters of the Third Republic, such as the immense triptyque by Puvis de Chavannes, representing *the Childhood of Sainte Geneviève*. In place of the alter, a gigantic plaster composition honors the National Convention.

The crypt is more moving. After the splendor and the grandiloquence of the nave, come the simple stone vaults and columns.

In this crypt a part of the grandeur of France reposes. Since 1795, the sarcophagi of Voltaire and Rousseau symbolically face each other. By this confrontation, the Revolution succeded in reconciling the two literary giants of the Enlightenment. Since then other associations for eternity have not been by chance! Victor Hugo reposes next to Zola; Jean Moulin, the resistance fighter of Second World War is next to Jean Monnet, the founder of modern Europe. Without the first, how could there have been the second?

The only manifestation of life daring to break the immobility and the silence of eternity is a screen on which is projected a film showing great contemporary events linked to the Panthéon. The shaking and cavernous voice of Malraux haunts this kingdom. "Return here, Jean Moulin, with your sad procession of those that were killed and still more tragic, those who spoke..." Then appears President Mitterrand on a certain May 21, 1981, offering a red rose to Jaurès, another to Jean Moulin, while Beethoven's *Hymn to Joy* fills the crypt. On this day, Paris was torn in two. Who would be the first to lay at rest in the eternal crypt – Malraux, Mitterrand, de Gaulle, or Pompidou.

Finally, do not forget to climb to the terrace of the dome where you can contemplate one of the most beautiful panoramas of Paris.

On the Place du Panthéon lovers of surrealism will not fail to stop before this monument. It is there that Breton, helped by Eluard, Aragon, Benjamin Péret and Philippe Soupault wrote the first issues of the magazine "Littérature".

A bit farther along the square at the top of the Rue de la Montagne Sainte-Geneviève, stands the church Saint-Étienne du Mont. It replaces a chapel which was part of the abbey Sainte-Geneviève. It took a hundred and thirty years to construct. Begun in 1492, it was completed only in 1626. The interior offers a diversity of astonishing styles, with its magnificent Renaissance "rood loft", unique in its kind, that illuminates superb stained glass windows of the XVIth and XVIIth centuries. Racine and Pascal are buried there, just a couple of steps from the Panthéon, separated forever from Voltaire and our great men. Verlaine died, alone and naked, on the floor of a neighbouring house in the Rue Descartes. His funeral mass – fifth class – took place in Saint-Étienne du Mont in the presence of Mallarmé, Barrès, François Coppée and Catulle-Mendès. Since 1806, a gilt vault shelters the stone sarcophagus of Sainte Geneviève who saved Paris from the hordes of Attila. Elevated to the rank of Patron Saint of the city, she was the object of a popular and fervent cult up until the XIXth century. When piety was rekindled in May, 1940, crowds once again implored the protection of this saint. Paul Léautaud preferred to ironize: *We have returned to the year* 1000.

From the Place du Panthéon, we reach the heart of the Latin Quarter, the center of Parisian teaching since the XIIth century. It was called the Latin Quarter because in the past only Latin was spoken there.

From this square, you reach the Sorbonne, the oldest university of Paris, via the Rue Soufflot. On the right, the Rue Victor Cousin is a prolongation of the Rue de la Sorbonne.

The Latin Quarter

The Latin Quarter roars regularly. Slingshot mentality, street battles, the student demonstrations are rituals there. The events of May, 1968, remain engraved in the memory of Paris. The government of the time trembled in its shoes. A completely new social order sprang from the cobble stones of Boulevard Saint-Michel and from the Rue Gay-Lussac. At least, a lot of people choose to think so.

So that such events never happened again, Général de Gaulle had the paving stones removed and then covered the boulevards and streets with asphalt. At the same time the National Education System proceeded to split up the Sorbonne into numerous educational units spread all across Paris and its suburbs. But nothing really happened. Students continue to frequent the cafés, the bookshops, the theatres and the cinemas of the Latin Quarter. But, on the other hand, how could it ever be otherwise? The most prestigious schools, the most famous schools of France have traditionally been located in this area. The Sorbonne, where "Letters" are taught, is of course the most known of the schools. But there is also the Faculty of Medicine, the College of France, the famous high schools Louis-le-Grand and Henri IV, the Polytechnic School and the "Ecole Normal Superior". If this is not enough, then one can add the school of Decorative Arts, the Faculty of Law, etc. The histories of these schools are so bound together it is impossible to say which one is the originator of their respective reputations.

It is estimated that more than twenty thousand students lived on the Montagne Sainte-Geneviève during the Middle Ages. Pope Innocence III allowed them to form a corporation which became the

47

University of Paris in 1215. In the year 1256, the canon Robert de Sorbon obtained authorisation from King Louis IX to found a college dedicated to teaching theology. It is thus that the Sorbonne was created, taking the name its founder. It would remain the center for theological study and the seat of the University of Paris until 1792, when it was closed down. Napoléon re-established it in 1806. It was renovated under the Third Republic by the architect Nénot and decorated by academic painters of the period, among them was Puvis de Chavannes. It was he who was responsible for the painting in the Grand Amphithéatre. It is the same university that we see today. The chapel, built between 1635 and 1653, on orders from Richelieu, houses the tomb of the cardinal. The French Academy celebrated its tricentenaire there in 1935.

A bit further on, beyond the Place de la Sorbonne, after crossing the Boul' Mich', as the Boulevard Saint-Michel is called, and walking several meters on the Rue de Vaugirard, you come to the Odéon. Inaugurated in 1782, to foster French Actors, this French Theatre has one of the largest seating capacities in Paris. T*he Marriage of Figaro* by Beaumarchais was created there in 1784. The theatre changed names several times in the course of history. Theatre of the Nation from 1790 to 1793, then Theatre of Equality in 1794. In 1797, it became the Odéon Theatre.

More recently the theatre, becoming the Theatre of France, was confided to the Jean-Louis Barrault and Madeleine Renaud troop in 1959. This troop of actors brought back the theatre's former luster. Claudel, Ionesco, Genet were all performed there. It was a wonderful period for the theatre until it was put to an end by the tumultuous occupation of the location by students in May, 1968. For ten years, the Odéon has been allied to the Comédie- Française and often features foreign productions.

The Place de l'Odéon has kept its XVIIIth century character. At number 1, the Café Voltaire has been replaced by the Benjamin Franklin American Library. This café was, at the height of symbolism, one of the busiest literary places in town. During the period between the wars it became the hub for American writers living in Paris. Writers such as Hemingway, Scott Fitzgerald, T.S. Eliot and Ezra Pound. T*he Méditerranée*, one of Cocteau's favorite restaurants, continues this literary tradition in a decor painted by the artist Bérard.

Saint-Germain-des-Prés

The village of Saint-Germain-des-Prés was a religious place long before the Existentialistes took over its cellars and the terraces of its cafés. In the VIth century, Germain, the bishop of Paris, decided to construct a basilica in the middle of the meadows on the left bank. This church was intended to house relics of the tunic of Saint Vincent, which had been brought from Spain by Chilibert, King of the Francs. A monastery was attached to the church and around it a village of peasants developed little by little. The village took the name of its sanctified bishop. Thus the village of Saint-Germain-des-Prés came into being.

In the VIIth century, the abbey became one of the most prosperous in the Benedictine order. It spread over a vast area of more than fifteen thousand hectares. Devastated four times by Norman invaders, it was entirely reconstructed between 990 and 1021. The present church dates from this period. The village continued to prosper. In the XIIIth century, it had its parish, Saint-Sulpice, its annual market, the fair Saint-Germain, and even a prison. From the XVIth century, private estates began to be constructed nearby, in what was to become the suburb Saint-Germain. In the XVIIth century, westward and to the south of the steeple, several streets were laid out, even within the abbey itself.

48

The area rapidly became a place for trade and strolling. It was in this period that the abbot in charge, the cardinal de Furstenberg, opened the charming Place de Furstenberg. Shaded by gracious trees, it still has its original buildings. The painter Delacroix resided in one of them, at number 6. His studio and apartment have been transformed into a museum.

A part of the abbey was used as a military prison during the French Revolution. The Swiss Guards that had escaped the slaughter of the Tuileries, which took place August 10, 1792, as well as refactory priests, were incarcerated there. On September 2, 1792, in the course of a riot, a cart carrying several of these priests to the prison was intercepted and its occupants slaughtered. In their vigor, the rioters lay sack to the prison and massacred all its prisoners. The slaughter continued for three days and ceased only on the fifth. There were no more victims to kill. More than three hundred corpses soaked the gardens of the abbey with blood. The prison was demolished in 1857, when work was begun laying out the Boulevard Saint-Germain.

The church of Saint-Germain-des-Prés is the oldest in Paris. It no longer resembles the romanesque church that Pope Alexandre III came to consecrate in 1163, however. Two of its three steeples have disappeared. The last floor of that which remains was redone in the XIXth century, its Roman porch is masked by a portal of the XVIth century and the rectory on the right was added in the XVIIIth century! The external architecture no longer illustrates the original Roman style.

The interior, worked over in the XIXth century, is even less authentic. The Revolution transformed the church into a saltpeter factory after having sacked it. The two towers of the transept were destroyed and the sculpted capitals of the nave were transferred to the Cluny Museum and were replaced by copies.

During the Second Empire at the instigation of Baltard, the frescoes of the arcades of the nave were painted by Hippolyte Flandrin, a pupil of Ingres. At the beginning of this century, iron grilles in the Art Deco style were placed so as to frame the choir. Chapels of the ambulatory constitute the most interesting part of the church. They contain the tombs of Boileau, Descartes and Mabillon, the Benedictine scholar to whom we owe the foundations of diplomacy.

The XIXth century made this village, as so many other quarters of Paris, the stage for another revolution, this time a peaceful one: that of Baron Haussmann. From 1852, and for about twenty years, the quarter lived only to the rhythm of orders from architects and urbanists, the sound of spades and pickaxes, constructions and demolitions, expulsions and relocations. The Boulevard Saint-Germain and the Rue de Rennes were laid out and the area around the church transformed. Dozens of private homes disappeared to make way for new ones, all aligned along the new avenues. When the work ended, the quarter once again took up the calm and serene way of life that it had almost always known.

It was on the eve of the war of 1914-1918 that Saint-Germain-des-Prés became a hotbed for intellectual revolution. It was a place of contention for the establishment and a center for student and artistic banter. There, one "lives, breathes, pulses and sleeps" by virtue of the three cafés as famous today as state institutions: The *Deux Magots*, the *Café de Flore* and the *Brasserie Lipp*, each one of which has its bureaucrats, its department heads and its lowly pencil pushers. "Those would be novelists translated into 26 languages, painters without studios, critics with no headlines to their names or ministers without portfolios", wrote Léon Paul Fargue.

Charles Maurras is perhaps the pioneer of political action in the quarter. He was upsetting French politics even before 1914 at the *Café de Flore* toward the end of the Second Empire, by drafting the first issues of "French Action" (*L'Action Française*) and by founding, in 1908, the political party of the same name.

"Evenings in Paris" (*Soirées de Paris*) founded by Apollinaire in 1912, united quite a group of people. When the poet presented the works of his painter friends, the cubists Braque and Picasso, on the terrace of a café, there was an enormous scandal. They were abused... and the critics denounced the non-painters... and certain subscribers of this review tore up their subscription cards as a sign of their displeasure.

After World War I, all these irreconcilables took up positions in their cafés and bistros, which served as their headquarters. The left and the extreme left took up their position at the *Café de Flore* while the extreme right held forth at the *Bistro Lipp*. The surrealists, at the instigation of André Breton, utilized the various galleries of the quarter to display their creative efforts. The openings of their expositions were always encircled by the hot breath of scandal.

At the *Café de Flore*, near the end of the 1930's, the get-togethers were led by the Prévert brothers, Marcel Duhamel, the founder of the Black Series (*Série Noire*), Jean-Louis Barrault and Roger Blin who rehearsed his *The Attic* in the Rue des Grands-Augustins. During the war, Sartre and Simone de Beauvoir hid out there and wrote their books which changed modern philosophy. Camus dropped by in the late afternoon and Picasso came at night. The budding poets, to get themselves inspired, sat in the tight group around Desnos and Prévert.

After the sudden Liberation, the quarter "exploded". Cellars and cabarets opened by tens attracting the youth of the day who crowded there each night. Artists, philosophers, musicians, poets, famous or anonymous, shared totally the happiness of a new-found freedom. Long hair, plaid shirts were the uniform of the youths who invaded the cellars filled with the music of jazz. Each one exhausted himself by dancing the *be-bop*. These were the mad, fun-filled nights between the *Tabou*, the *Vieux Colombier*, the *Rose Rouge*, the *Lorientais*, the *Fontaine des Quatre Saisons* or the *Club Saint-Germain*. During the day the jazz bands of the Beaux-Arts cavorted in the streets to *New Orleans* style music.

The period, as sudden as it was surprising had to have an identity. It was labeled *existentialiste*. Daniel Gélin remembers the origin of this label which became indissociable with Saint-Germain-des-Prés. "One of my friends, a journalist for an evening newspaper, Jacques Robert, once had the delicate assignment to write an article on the *Tabou*. The article was to have photographs of the club as well. He was to describe the youth that gathered there and what inspired them. Once the article was written he needed a catchy title to fit into a certain number of spaces left above the column. He was a gifted writer and he could conceive and finish an article quickly. He was also very cultured, he knew the influence of Kierkegaard, Heidegger, Husserl and Hegel, author of *Critique de la Raison Dialectique*. As it turned out the word *existentialisme* fit perfectly in the space reserved for his title. And it is thus that these young people – dressed more comfortably to dance easier (plaid shirts to absorb sweat, tennis shoes to jump higher) – were given this expression, which has been attributed to me because of my 'Sartre connections'."

The list of personalities that participated in this happy collective madness would be tedious to enumerate. Behind the unclassifiable queens of the quarter, Juliette Gréco and Annabel, is an incredible list of stars who performed there: writers such as Sartre, Camus, Beauvoir,

Prévert, Raymond Queneau, Malaparte, Jacques udiberti, Boris Vian film directors Roger Vadim, Orson Welles, Jean Renoir, Jacques Becker, painters such as Foujita, actors such as Gérard Philipe, Simone Signoret, Yves Montand, Odile Versois, Daniel Gélin, Michel Piccoli, Yves Robert, Marlene Dietrich and Jean Gabin, singers like Mouloudji and Léo Ferré. All united around the cult of jazz, whose high priests were Django Reinhardt, Claude Luter, Moustache, Sidney Bechet, Duke Ellington, Stéphane Grapelli... and Boris Vian. An eclectic crowd coming together with the same urgency to live, to create and to laugh.

It was Bohemian happiness for broke and carefree people when there was everything to conquer and solidarity was still the law of artists. To blossom, momentarily there, between the *Flore*, the *Deux Magots* and *Lipp*, in the shadow of the church Saint-Germain-des-Prés was wonderful. What is the secret of these places? Without doubt it is recorded in this scrap of telephone conversation between Daniel Gélin and Juliette Gréco, who, in 1993, recalls her debut:
Juliette: ... That was the beginning, with my three songs by Sartre, Queneau and Desnos, with music by Kosma...
Daniel Gélin: ... I remember that, each evening, we all had as much stage fright as you!
Juliette: Ah, how kind you are!
Daniel Gélin: We had fun! Hey, didn't we have fun?
Juliette: Ah yes, what fun we had...
Today in Saint-Germain, ready-to-wear clothes shops have unfortunately replaced a lot of the cafés, cinemas and book shops. Some still resist the change and how good it is to leaf through a book at *La Hune* or the *Divan* and how lovely to have breakfast at the *Flore* or dinner at *Lipp*.

The Institut de France

When he died, in 1661, Mazarin left a large sum of money in his will to create an institution open to sixty students born in the four provinces annexed to France by the treaties of Westphalie (1648) and The Pyrenees (1659). To be exact: Artois, Alsace, the Piémont and the Roussillon.
Louis Le Vau was assigned the task. Begun in 1663, construction lasted more than twenty years. The tour de Nesles had to be pulled down. It was on the site of the institute. Queen Jeanne of Burgundy had made it famous. Widow of the king of France, Philippe V (1293-1322), she came to live in the Nesles mansion whose tower advanced over the Seine. From there, Brantôme tells us she "lay in wait for passers-by and those that pleased her were invited to come up to see her, and once having her way with them, had them thrown from the tower down into the water".
In 1684, the College of the Four Nations (Collège des Quatre Nations) finally opened its doors to its young students. The remains of Mazarin, as well as his extensive library, the Mazarine, were immediately transferred there. In the center of the elegant curved façade which faces the Seine, Le Vau had a high-domed chapel erected.
The College was closed during the Revolution, to become, in 1793, a prison.
It was at the initiative of Napoléon, that the Institute was transferred to the College of the Four Nations in 1806. Founded eleven years previously, it regrouped the French Academy (created in 1635 by Richelieu), the Academy of Inscriptions and Fine Arts, the Academy of Letters, the Academy of Science and the Academy of Moral and Political Sciences. The chapel became the place for ceremonies of the French Academy and reception speeches still resonate under its famous dome. The immortals, as members of the French Academy are called – whose motto is: "To

immortality" – are only forty in number. Only on the death of one of its members can a new immortal be elected. It is easy enough to venture into the courtyard of the Institute. With a little luck, some Thursday, the day for ceremonies, you may see the forty members resting there a moment to smoke a cigarette, with a strange bicorne hat jammed under the arm, dressed in the famous green outfit with a sword at the side. Gods actually do speak of mortal things after all.

The Luxemburg Gardens and the Senate

At the demand of Marie de Médicis, in 1613, Salomon de Brosse designed the palace and gardens of Luxemburg on a terrain that the Italian had bought from the Duke of Luxemburg. The grounds and buildings were inspired by the Pitti Palace in Florence. The palace is today the seat of the Senate.

On this terrain, Robert le Pieux, King of France from 996 to 1031, had Vauvert construct a castle to use as a retreat after being excommunicated by the pope for having repudiated his wife. Legend has it that his castle was haunted by demons. From this legend come the expressions: "go to the devil Vauvert" and by contraction: "go to the devil". In reality, it seems more likely that the property was inhabited by rogues whose nocturnal goings-on and disguises scared the neighbourhood.

With its multi-levels, its large lawns, its walkways and terraces, pools and fountains, the gardens became, from the very start, both the "lung" of the Latin Quarter and a playground for students. "How many novels were started and outlined there and ended at the *Closerie des Lilas!*" wrote Alfred Delvau. "How many maidens have come to sit on the benches... of the Grand Walkway, in the company of young aspiring attornies or physicians, to get up together after an hour or so of amourous chat!..." At the Médicis fountain, that eternal rendez-vous of lovers, the jealous Polyphème stands ready to crush Acis, who holds the object of his desires in his arms – the lovely sea nymphe Galathée. Luxemburg gardens carry moving memories of many a writer and artist who spent a great part of their youth there, having lived in the quarter. Such names as André Gide, who as a child, lived in the Rue Médicis and sailed his toy boats in the large pool. Many famous people have even studied their lessons in these gardens. The shadows of Victor Hugo still glide through the gardens; also those of Alfred de Musset who sang its praises: "... charming place, solitary asylum." Baudelaire came to stroll there with Théodore de Banville, Maupassant found it "pretty as a sweet old smile" and Lamartine met Sainte-Beuve there. The list would be long of those writers who worked in the Senate, such as François Coppée, Anatole France and Leconte de Lisle, Verlaine, when he resided in the Rue Descartes, or Hemingway who, in the evening, caught pigeons in the garden to make a meal.

Today, once again, lovers, students and young mothers cross each other in the lanes of the "Luco", little boats float in the fountain pool, old folks talk and argue. Not far from the merry-go-round people still go bowling and the small Guignol (puppet) theatre is an institution through the generations. The gardens still remain today what they have always been. On the eve of the Second World War, Brasillach wrote this strange saying: "In the month of June, when I cross Luxemburg, I always look at the young people and the young girls seated on the iron chairs, under stone statues of queens. We were similar to them, we dragged through warm days, our history notebooks with us. Under the trees we worked in the open air, softened suddenly by a puff of scented air..."

Montparnasse

Montparnasse remains a myth... but Montparnasse is a myth only. If this quarter was for ten years called "crazy", one of the most active artistic centers of Paris, it is unfortunately no more than a faded memory of former times. The quarter has been totally transformed, disfigured, and one has to look hard for the last vestiges of those years in *La Coupole*, in the *Dome*, in *The Rotonde* and at the *Sélect*, cafés that were part of the madness of the beginning of the century. But for the rest, everything has been ruined. The ugliness of the new train station, the pretentious Montparnasse tower and the banality of the shopping center that goes with it, make one long bitterly for the decor of the past. Paris no longer is a feast in Montparnasse; and *La Palette*, a bistro frequented by all the illustratrious *montparnos*, has become a steak house, a sad illustration of the standardization without a soul of capital cities. From 1918 until the Crash of 1929, every artist who had the least bit of ambition had to live in Montparnasse. They came there trying to make ends meet and participate in this permanent feast. A party that never stopped, day or night. Some *montparnos* became famous. Some examples are: Max Jacob, Picasso, Foujita, Picabia, Blaise Cendrars, Kisling, André Salmon, Derain, Modigliani, Pascin, Ernest Hemingway and Fitzgerald! The surrealists, before taking to the boulevards, also frequented Montparnasse. Breton and Tzara were regulars of *The Closerie*. An artist's consecration passed through this "village". Milestones of this group were the modest cafés where each one could keep warm in winter and sometimes eat without it costing too much: *The Closerie des Lilas* to the north, *La Coupole* and the *Dome* to the south. Come nightfall, in the dim light of the *Jockey*, a club where everyone met in the evening, they listened to *Kiki de Montparnasse*, in the middle of an indescribable hub-bub.

Unbuttoned to the waist, she sang baudy songs. During the day she posed for her friends. "The orgy is in Montparnasse", Max Jacob announced triomphantly. The music of the islands, Hawaii and Martinique, gave rhythm, noted a journalist, even if "Negro music grates on the nerves". We still have the extraordinary photographs of Man Ray, famous paintings, the works of Hemingway, Cendrars and many others.

But Montparnasse soon clouded over. In January, 1920, Modigliani, gnawed by alcohol and gaunt from misery, died in the hospital. His friend, desperate, threw herself from a window. Nine years later, recalls Pierre Cabanne, Madeleine Anspach, whose husband had made a fortune, "gave an even more tumultuous party than was usual in the *Bal Nègre* in the Rue Blomet. Two days after, the Wall Street Crash came, and the Americans quickly left and there was general panic for all the others. From one day to the next, painters' quotations collapsed, merchants folded up and 'Mado', went back to Belgium... and committed suicide... The party was over."

The Invalides

The dome of Les Invalides shines once again in the Paris sky. Its decoration of garlands, trophies and floral motifs found their gold again in July, 1989, on the occasion of the bi-centenial of the French Revolution. A welcome initiative that allows us to discover it such as Parisians saw it in Louis XIV's century. The Sun King wanted to build a hospital worthy of the sacrifices and courage of his soldiers. The vast terrain of Grenelle was chosen to put up this monument and Libéral Bruant directed construction from 1671 to 1676, before Hardouin Mansart made the dome which was finished in 1706. The king wrote in his will: "Of all the different projects we have accomplished, there is none more useful to the State than that of Les Invalides."

There is none other more successful for its indisputable humanistic intention and for its architectural success. Montesquieu said of Les Invalides that it was "the most respectable place on earth", before adding, "I would like to have made this monument, if I were a prince, more than to have won three battles." Today, besides the hospital buildings and the military government of Paris, Les Invalides house the Museum of the Army, the Museum of the Liberation, The Veterans Office and Napoléon's tomb.

It was Louis-Philippe who decided to return the remains of Napoléon I to France. The reason for this gesture was very political. Son of Philippe Égalité, he was detested by monarchists as much as by republicans. He therefore had to seduce the bonapartists who were still very numerous in France.

His son, the Duke of Joinville, was sent to collect the emperor's remains from Sainte-Hélène. Upon his return, the prince rode with the coffin from Courbevoie to the Arc of Triumph where the official parade began. A huge crowd pressed on the way from the Étoile to the Invalides. The son of the king led the procession which was headed by a gigantic chariot drawn by eight horses. On top of the chariot was placed the coffin. Victor Hugo, who was a witness, recalled: "It was very cold, with a beautiful sun; light hazes hung in the sky. Brooks were frozen... the canon at the city hall went off every quarter of an hour. The crowd trampled and shuffled... At the end of the Esplanade, towards the river, a double row of guards on horseback, with splendid uniforms, waited solemnly. The procession, full of generals and marshals was an admirable sight... The chariot stopped. It was a huge mass entirely gilded, rising like a pyramid above the four golden wheels which carried it. Two immense beams of flags from all the nations of Europe flew with magnificence in front and behind the chariot... The Prince of Joinville told the king: 'Sire, I present you the body of the Emperor Napoléon.' The king replied: 'I receive it in the name of France.'"

The remains of Napoléon thus entered the Invalides where a circular crypt had been prepared to receive the red porphyry that rests on a base of green granit from the Vosges mountains. On December 15, 1940, a century later, day for day, the body of the Duke of Reichstadt, the son of Napoléon whom Rostand baptized "Aiglon" (little eagle) entered a "cella" of the crypt, beside the statue of the Emperor in full uniform.

The Gare d'Orsay

On the quay Anatole France, the former Orsay train station has housed the Museum of the XIXth Century since 1986. It was decided to display, in the same place, all the relative collections of that century – as rich as they are varied. Collections from the Louvre and the Jeu de Paume are presented here. The station was renovated, thus preserving one of the last examples of industrial architecture by Victor Laloux, who erected it from 1898 to 1900. "The station is superb and looks like a Palace of Fine Arts", had joked his painter friend and visionary, Édouard Detaille, on the day of its opening.

This station disgorged passengers arriving from the Southwest via the Austerlitz station. It rapidly became too small and was closed in 1939. In reality, it was used one last time, in 1945, when it was used to disembark, under its majestic glass windows, survivors of the death camps who revealed to a liberated Paris the atrocities that they had suffered, unknown in the city up to that time. Then it was marked for destruction, to be replaced by a gigantic and impersonal complex of offices and hotels. The banality of the projects presented and administrative red tape saved it from the worst. While waiting for a decision, the station was confided in part to the theatrical troup of Renaud-Barrault, after they had been moved out of the Odéon. The rest of it was allocated to Drouot-Left Bank, a public auction house. The sudden infatuation with industrial architecture that surfaced after the destruction of Les Halles de Baltard, fired the idea of creating a museum in this place, which had been classified as a historical monument in 1978. For this reason Pierre Cabanne could write "the Orsay station becomes the temple of repentance".

This museum brings together art of the XIXth century, or more exactly all artistic creation from approximately 1848 to 1914, and bridges the gap between the Louvre and the Center Georges Pompidou. Paintings first: without discrimination we find the heaviness of Cabanel or Cormon and the pomp of the Belle Époque, the elegance of Degas, the naturalism of Daumier, the light of the impressionists, Manet, Monet, Renoir or Pissarro, as well as superb rooms devoted to Nabis, or Fauves. The sculpture is dominated by the grace of works by Carpeaux. The original of his work *The Dance* adorns the façade of the Paris Opera. This temple of iron and glass illustrates architecture of the applied arts, from the decorative arts of the Second Empire to the very rich Art Nouveau collections. They all find a fitting place. The same goes for photography and the cinema which came into being in the course of this eclectic century where art and technique came together.

Facing the entry to the Museum, behind grilles, you can see a delightful building of the XVIIIth century: the *Legion of Honor*, whose majestic entry is situated at Number 64, Rue de Lille.
It was built on the initiative of a prince as prodigal as he was original: Frédéric Othon, Prince of Salm Kyrburg. He acquired the land in 1781 from the Prince of Conti. It was a marshy terrain that served to store wood brought in by boats. This ground, which was soft and often flooded, slowed down construction and cost the proprietor most of his principality. Only after selling the three villages that he possessed in the Vosges was he able to finish construction. Towards the end of 1786 it was finally inaugurated.

Although a foreigner, he refused to leave Paris in 1789. Better yet, he enrolled in the National Guard where he became a captain and converted his residence into a club. "He baptized it *Salmigondis*, a nickname recalling both the name of the owner and limpidity of the club members' controversy", reports Georges Cain.

These revolutionary inclinations did not bring him luck, since the General Security Committee launched a decree to arrest the "Citizen Salm, this foreign prince, for being, under the mask of patriotism, a secret agent for the German coalition against France". The prince was beheaded a bit later on, at the place du Trône.

After having become briefly the property of a wig maker that the revolution had made rich, the building became the property of Mme de Staël. It was there that she brought together her friends from the Constitutional Club, before being exhiled by the First Consul.

After that, Napoléon created the Legion of Honor. The great Chancery and officies in the Order were installed and remain there today.

The building was looted, then burnt by the "Communards". Its reparation was entirely financed by a voluntary contribution of the 65,000 members in the Order. In the part added in the XIXth century, one can visit the Museum of the Legion of Honor and the Order of Chivalry, where royal orders, Napoléonic souvenirs, uniforms, decorations, paintings, a collection of foreign medals and contemporary decoration medals are displayed.

The Louvre

Seven centuries were necessary to construct and finish the Louvre. From its completion in 1200 to the construction of the pyramid of Pei, it tells in its own way about the ambitions and vicissitudes of those who have dominated France.

One after the other, these powerful men have left their imprint on this monument of Paris that is far more than just the largest museum in the world.

Each in his turn, Philippe Auguste, Louis IX, Charles V, François I, Henri II, Catherine de Médicis, Henri IV, Marie de Médicis, Louis XIII, Louis XIV, Colbert, Louis XVI, the Revolutionaries of 1789, Napoléon I, Napoléon III, the Communards, the Third Republic and last of all Mitterrand have all enlarged, modified, destroyed, reconstructed, reorganized and made of it a symbol of political intrigue. All this makes up the museum that we see today. The history of France and that of Paris are both written in each of its stones. The history of our architecture also! The greatest architects worked on it. For examples we can list: Jean Gudgeon, Philibert Delorme, Jacques Lemercier, Le Vau, Le Bernin, Claude Perrault, Le Brun, Fontaine and Percier, Visconti and recently Pei.

From the Gothic, under the influence of François I, came the Renaissance style. The high colonnade by Perrault in the XVIIth century is a masterpiece of classicism and the Richelieu wing built under the Second Empire contains the private quarters of the Emperor which reflect the purest Napoléon III style.

The Cour carrée (the square courtyard) constitutes the oldest part of the present day Louvre. It was built on the site of the fortress built in the XIIIth century by Philippe Auguste. In its center, the Pavilion of the Clock, a work by Lemercier dates from 1624. Splendid caryatids overhang a clock put in place during the Restoration. To the west is the admirable pavilion built by Pierre Lescot, under the reign of François I, adorned by the sculptures of Jean Gudgeon. It is a true masterpiece of Renaissance architecture in Paris. By the door of the main entry, which gives onto the Place du Louvre, one sees the tower that was built under the Second Empire, between the City Hall of the first "arrondissement" and the church Saint-Germain l'Auxerrois. This admirable XIIth century church was constantly modified until the XVIth century. It is linked to the tragic memory of the Saint-Barthélemy, a night of religious madness, when Catholics had decided to exterminate Protestants. In the somber night of August 23, 1572, bells of this church rang out, giving the signal for the massacre that in three days accounted for more than 3,000 victims and plunged France into a civil war.

Recent works to complete the Great Louvre have brought to light vestiges of the medieval Louvre – the dungeon and trenches of Philippe Auguste's castle and the foundations of the north and east wings that Charles V replaced. This underground stroll is magnificent.

It is on the *place du Carrousel* that in June, 1662, the Great Carrousel (the Great Race) that gave the place its name, took place. Fifteen thousand spectators surrounded the track where five grids with ten horsemen each were poised. Louis XIV gave orders to the Romans, all decked out in gold. His brother commanded the Persians, who were dressed in silver; the Prince of Condé ordered the Turks that were in blue and black; the Duke of Enghien directed multicolored Indians; the Duke of Guise commanded the Americans, who were in green and amarant. All were contestants in the races. Prizes were diamonds given to the victors by princesses. The twenty-four years old king must have been vexed not to have given the highest prizes himself.

The *Arc de Triomphe du Carrousel* is situated in the heart of the Place du Carrousel. It opens onto the Tuileries gardens, and continuing the perspective, is the obelisk of Luxor and the Arc of Triumph of the Étoile. It was erected in 1808 according to plans drawn by Percier and Fontaine. They had copied with humor the Arc of Constantine in Rome. Built when the Empire was in all its splendor, it celebrates the great victories: Austerlitz, Tilsitt, Ulm, etc. On its summit are the horses of Saint Mark which were triumphantly transported from Venice with other war trophies. The sculptor Lescot had harnessed them to a chariot containing the figures of War and Peace. But in 1815, after Napoléon's defeat, the Venetians recovered their horses and returned them to Venice. A work by the sculptor Bosio, placed there in 1820, represents the Restoration atop a chariot drawn by four horses. Initially, the quadriga that adorned Saint Mark in Venice and brought by the Emperor during his Italian campaigns, crowned it. The Venetians got it back in 1815. It is a replica of this quadriga that crowns the Arc today. It was made in 1828 by the sculptor Bosio.

The cultural dimension of the *Louvre Museum* is an ancient tradition. Even in the time of Charles V, by installing his library there, he gave the Louvre its first collections. François I brought the first paintings of the masters there: Raphael, Titian and Leonardo da Vinci. There were close to 200 paintings at the time of Henri IV, and 2,500 under the reign of Louis XIV! When he left the Louvre for Versailles, the palace was taken over by the five Academies. The court and the king no longer residing there, official artists settled in with their families and their servants. Pierre Cabanne tells us: "Partitions were erected and walls were pierced to make way for stove pipes. Large rooms were cut up, staircases were draughty and in all this mess, where, under kings, history had

been made, this heterogeneous group of parasites went so far as to install dance halls and cabarets on the ground floor. Hangars were constructed against the colonnade, a sort of flea market was set up in the Cour carrée. These people attracted every manner of thief, con-man and prostitute." It was in 1754 that these tenants were ousted, all except the academics, who were expulsed only fifty years later by Napoléon I, who needed the palace... to celebrate his wedding.

The French Revolution transformed the Louvre into a museum. It was then called *the palace of the people*. It was opened to the public in 1793. The conquests of Napoléon enriched it with works from all over the world... that had to be given back in 1815. Only *The Marriage of Cane* was not returned. This Venitian masterpiece had been judged too large to be transported! Louis XVIII and Charles X are responsable for the Egyptian, Greek and Assyrian antiquity collections. These as well as the Roman antiquities were acquired under their reign. Since the XIXth century, acquisitions have continued to increase and diversify. They number today more than 400,000.

In September, 1981, President Mitterrand decided to make the Louvre the largest museum in the world. The Ministry of Finance was therefore moved to Bercy so as to liberate the Richelieu wing where it had been since the end of the XIXth century. The Chinese-American architect Icoh Ming Pei was hired to reorganize the museum. The exhibition surface of the museum doubled (60,000 square meters today) and the nineteen meter high glass pyramid was built in the Napoléon courtyard. This is now the main entry and was very controversial. The idea appeared absurd to construct a structure that partly hides the façades, in spite of the transparency of its glass, of this historic building. Nevertheless, this pyramid is a continuation of forgotten projects. In 1794, on the same spot, there had already been an ephemeral pyramid built in memory of "the virtuous Marat", assassinated the preceding year. Then in 1809, Balzac's father had proposed to raise a pyramid, "in the middle of the great courtyard between the Tuileries and the Louvre" to honor Napoléon, which would have been topped by a monumental statue of the Emperor.

All subjective consideration aside, we do not miss the parking lots and coaches that the pyramid replaced.

The Tuileries

Catherine de Médicis, escaping the old Louvre, had the Palace of the Tuileries built. It no longer remains, since it was burned by the Communards in 1871. All that is left are the Flora pavilion on the quay of the Tuileries, and the Marsan pavilion, that today houses the Decorative Arts Museum, on the Rue de Rivoli.

In front of this palace she had drawn, in the Italian style, a garden with fountains, labyrinths of greenery, pools and statues. A menagerie and an artificial cave particularly attracted the Parisians, as access to the garden was free. Henri IV added a greenhouse.

Le Nôtre redesigned it in the French style in 1644. Up to the current transformation, the Tuileries gardens have constantly been modified to suit the tastes of landscape artists. The gardens still remain a favorite promenade for Parisians. Colbert wanted it reserved for the exclusive pleasure and use of the royal family but Charles Perrault, the author of A Book of Tales, the father of Tom Thumb and of Cinderella, pleaded for Parisians so well that the minister forgot his first intentions. Ever since, in the gardens, a bust of Perrault evokes the gratitude of strollers.

The stable that was built on the Terrace Feuillants, on the Rivoli side, for Louis XV when he was a child, no longer exists. On a morning of rioting, August 10, 1792, Louis XVI and his family were brought there, while the insurgent people took over the palace after having massacred the Swiss Guards. This was the beginning of the long series of troubles for the royal family. The king would return to this stable to be judged there and condemned to death. The guillotine was erected just a couple of steps away on the Place de la Révolution – the present day Place de la Concorde. It was once again in this stable that the Republic was instituted on September 21, 1792. It was destroyed in the XIXth century, during the First Empire when Rue de Rivoli was laid out. A plaque marks the site of this place today. It is on the grille of the gardens, opposite the entry to the Hôtel Meurice. According to Louis XVI, the garden had become in the XVIIIth century the place "of many indessencies". It was then made off-limits to prostitutes. Marchand took the opportunity to write The Lament of the Girls Who Are Forbidden Entry to the Tuileries, a book which had great success and in which these "ladies" sang ... in a quiet and somber retreat / Far from the trade of men / The charitable god of the gardens / favored us with its shade / So we wouldn't scandalize the neighbours... / But alas, the police inspectors / denounced us to their chiefs and / now this inhuman law / takes away our livelihood...

Another "indecency", a row of yew trees was used by stollers as public latrines, which were very rare at that time. In the zeal of cleaning things up, the trees were pulled up. This was an outrage that Sébastien Mercier tells of in his "Portrait of Paris", in 1783: "Formerly the Tuileries gardens were a meeting place for everyone. Those with urgent "needs" went under a hedge of yew trees and there they eased their needs... The Count of Angiviller, by pulling up these trees, ousted "pissers" that came with a deliberate and urgent purpose. Parisians quickly turned to the river banks." And he added: "Today, the river banks should be a pretty strolling area, but instead are revolting to the eye as well as to the nose."

Two museums, situated on the terrace that overlooks the Place de la Concorde, punctuate the gardens. The *Jeu de Paume*, that dates from the Second Empire, whose recent renovation has taken away its charm, is used for temporary exhibitions of contemporary art. The *Orangerie* houses the collection of an art dealer of the 1930's, Paul Guillaume. The collection was continued by his widow and her second husband, Jean Walter. It includes works of Cézanne, Renoir, Le Douanier Rousseau, Matisse, Picasso, Soutine, Modigliani, Derin, Utrillo, etc. In the basement, vast rooms contain the great mural decorations executed by Monet at the end of his life: *Nymphéas*. The murals have been there since 1927.

On November 11, 1918, Armistice Day, Monet wrote to Clemenceau to tell him he would give two panels of Nymphéas to the State. "It is a small thing, but it is the only way I have to share in the victory." It was because of this that the Orangerie of the Tuileries was especially arranged to his specifications. Monet agreed to this arrangement on condition that the murals be installed only after his death. He continued retouching them until the end. This calm and secret chapel where the *Nymphéas* remain, aroused eulogies from the beginning. Paul Claudel, one of the first visitors, noted in 1927: "Monet, at the end of his long life... has finished by treating the sweetest of all the elements, the most penetrable: water. It is not only transparent but a mirror as well. Thanks to water, he has painted what we can not see."

The Palais-Royal

Near the Louvre on the other side of the Rue de Rivoli, is one of the most beautiful, history-filled and most secret of places in Paris: the Palais-Royal. It is a garden and a palace at the same time. It was first the property of Richelieu, then of the family d'Orléans. Today it is the seat of the Council of State. It was the cradle of the French Revolution, then the "center" of Paris from 1800 to 1830. In its gardens, under its arcades or in the shade of its chestnut trees, mad animation reigned. Prostitutes and gamblers, aristocrats and revolutionaries, poets and financiers, bourgeois and players, young and old, Parisians or provincials, victors and the conquered from the past century were all there, side by side, jostling, drinking and fighting duels.

The Palace was first of all Richelieu's, then, on his death, he bequeathed it to Louis XIII. And thus the Cardinal Palace became the Royal Palace. Louis XIII gave it to his brother, the Duke of Chartres, of the House of Orléans. It was Philippe d'Orléans, cousin of Louis XVI who, in 1780, constructed the three wings that fringe the garden, and along them the streets named Rue de Valois, Rue de Beaujolais and Rue de Montpensier. These new buildings, a purely speculative operation, were destined to be sold. They had no other purpose but to fill this prince's empty coffers. His needs for money knew no limits. At the same time wooden shacks were built opposite the Palace, that were rented to various merchants and which attracted the whole of Paris at first, then all of Europe, a very mixed lot. In *Lost Illusions*, Balzac gives us a precise description of what was soon called the *Camp of Tartars*. "Small, quite badly covered huts, badly lit on the court side and on the garden side by daylight. They resembled the dirtiest of dance halls... These pigeon-holes had become so expensive as a result of all the crowds, that despite the tightness of some, their rental cost a thousand ecus... For twenty years the Stock Exchange was located on the ground floor of the Palace, just opposite. Appointments were made in these galleries before and after the market. The Paris of bankers and merchants often filled the courtyard of the Palais-Royal, and backed up under these shelters when it rained. Bursts of laughter abounded. There was never a quarrel at one end that was not known at the other end. There were booksellers, poetry, politics and prose, clothes sellers and, finally the 'ladies of the night' who came there only in the evening..."

It was in this happy atmosphere that the Revolution was fomented. The Duke d'Orléans, allergic to everyone who wore a kepis, forbade the access to his Palace and its garden to all policemen. Camille Desmoulins, Robespierre, Barras, Saint-Just, and the like, felt all the more at ease in this garden to spread their ideas. The duke himself considered it a pleasure to invite them to lunch in restaurants that had sprung up nearby: restaurants such as Frères Provençaux or the Café de Chartres. Thus on July 13, 1789, Camille Desmoulins urged the crowd to take up arms against the royalty. He pulled a leaf from a tree of the Palais-Royal and stuck it in his hat. This gesture, imitated by so many others, served as a rallying sign to the revolutionaries. The rosette of Desmoulins was not yet red, white and blue, but green... the color of hope! They all finished, nevertheless, on the guillotine. The Duke d'Orléans like the others, did not escape this fate. He had uselessly taken the precautions of being rebaptized Philippe Égalité, to call his property the Palace Égalité and to vote in favor of the death of his cousin the king!

When his son Louis Philippe d'Orléans became King of the French, in 1803, he decided to destroy these *wooden galleries* and chase away the prostitutes and gamblers who swarmed around the Palais-Royal. Even despite the superb *Glass Gallery* that Fontaine constructed on the ruins of the "Camp of Tartars", the population deserted the Palais-Royal to amuse themselves on the boulevards and in the neighbouring arcades. The Palais-Royal never recovered and slipped into a deep lethargy that still lingers.

Strollers are so rare today that it seems that Parisians and tourists have forgotten it. The Palais-Royal drowses between its superb façades designed by Louis at the end of the XVIIIth century. "That noise... did you hear it? A discrete low noise... This is nothing, it is only the Palais-Royal melting. Do not worry... it has been melting for a long time", wrote one of its more illustrious tenants: Colette.

Nevertheless, for some years now, commercial activity seems to have started up again. Several restaurants have opened recently, *Le Champagne*, which has been added to the very old restaurant, *Véfour* (which was called the *Café de Chartres* under the Revolution). "If one paved the gardens of the Palais-Royal, it would become our Saint Marc's Square", Cocteau liked to say, "And the *Véfour*... would be the *Café Florian* in this village called Paris, a village where leisure plays a considerable role." In the *Véfour*, you dine among shades of Fabre d'Églantine, Saint-Just, Bonaparte, Barras, Rastignac, also those of Colette, Cocteau, Marais, Morand and Giraudoux. This same Giraudoux who, while nonchalantly walking through the gardens, raised his arm and, pointing to a window, said to his dog: "Say hello to Mme Colette!"

Under the arcades can be found art galleries, modern sculpture galleries, galleries selling candles, porcelain dishes, fashions and jewels... but also galleries devoted to myths of the place such as the *Arcade Colette* that Jean-Claude Saladin devotes entirely to the memory of the writer that noted in *Three, Six, Nine*: "I like to think that a spell preserves the Palais-Royal: it collapses and yet remains, it disintegrates and does not move."

Not far away, *Shiseido*, in a neo-directoire gallery, sells precious perfumes. And the ageless windows display rows of withered decorations, medals and souvenirs of passed glories, rare stamps, etchings and canvases for those who favor "petit point".

The gardens have recently been spruced up, so much the better. But what has been placed in the elegant courtyard of the Palace? These columns designed by Buren, with red and green lighting which makes the place look like the runway of an airport? Cynics say that only dogs find them charming. The barbarity in urban design does not consist solely in destroying or burning... How sad that the money spent on these bi-colored posts had not been used to rebuild the former *Glass Gallery* of Louis Philippe which today is no more than stone colonnades.

Near the Palais-Royal, other cryptic places have managed to keep their charm from the past century: The arcades, the gallery Vivienne, the gallery Colbert, the gallery Véro-Dodat, and a bit farther on, the arcade of the Panoramas, all these were quite in vogue with Parisians after the decline of the Palais-Royal. They have recently come alive again. What a pleasure to stroll through the galleries where ghostly memories of Lautréamont, Verlaine, Baudelaire mix with those of Breton, Céline and Aragon. You have to climb the great staircase of the gallery Vivienne that leads to the courtyard of the Rue des Petits-Champs and continues to the home of Vidocq, the famous police burglar. "A modern peculiar light dominates this sort of covered gallery... it gleams almost like an underwater light, which, with sudden clarity, shines like a leg under a skirt that one catches a glimpse of", wrote Aragon.

The Place de la Concorde

Ditches originally separated the Tuileries gardens and the Place de la Concorde, once called the Place Louis XV. Today a parking lot has replaced these ditches. This square was built on former swamps between 1757 and 1772, under the reign of Louis XV. It has changed names seven times. Originally called the place Louis XV, it took the name of Place de la Révolution in 1792, Place de la Concorde in 1795, Louis XV again in 1814, Louis XVI in 1826, Louis XV again in 1828, only to be renamed Place de la Concorde in 1830, the name that it has kept ever since.

In 1748, the city of Paris decided to dedicate a place to its king, Louis XV "the beloved", in the center of which an equestrian statue was to be raised. The vast terrain situated between the Tuileries gardens and the Champs-Élysées was chosen as the site. The king's marble supply was stored there at that time. In this period, only the Cours la Reine and the banks of the Seine were fit for public use, as the Concorde Bridge over the river had not yet been built. The Rue Royale was only a mud path and the Champs-Élysées only a disreputable row of trees and vegetables gardens. In June, 1757, the king finally accepted the project proposed by Gabriel. The equestrian statue was confided to Bouchardon. On the pedestal, four allegorical statues representing Force, Justice, Peace and Prudence were planned. The inauguration of the square took place in 1763. The king had lost a lot of his prestige, to the point that people sang: "Ah! the beautiful statue, ah! the beautiful pedestal, Virtues are on foot, and Vice is on the horse!"

On May 30, 1770, the place Louis XV was the stage of a dreadful catastrophe, a disastrous sign of destiny. On this day the marriage of the dolphin, the future Louis XVI, and the archduchess of Austria, Marie-Antoinette, was celebrated. A fireworks display was held for the immense crowd when a rocket, badly aimed, started a fire in the temple of Hymen, which had been erected for the ceremony. An indescribable panic ensued. Everyone clamoured for the exits. Georges Cain tells us: "On the side of the Seine, those trying to escape fell into the river; the bridge did not yet exist. Others tried to escape by the Rue Royale but this street was encumbered, obstructed by construction materials. The ground was dug up and full of building stone of great size which made the way dangerous and almost impracticable; it was there, however, that the crowd headed, screaming with the impetuosity of a torrent. They were crushed and others were forced to walk over the dead and the dying. The next day, a hundred and thirty-three corpses gathered from the ground were laid out on the square, and more than three hundred victims died later on from their injuries."

This event remained engraved in the memory of the people of Paris for a long time. Twenty years later, these two martyrs were beheaded on the same spot where they were married.

In August, 1792, the statue of Louis XV was pulled down and replaced by a colossal statue of Liberty. On January 21, 1793, the guillotine was set up on this Place de la Révolution to behead Louis XVI. For eighteen months it would stand on the square. More than a thousand persons perished there, under the cleaver of the "great national razor".

The executioner Sanson told of the agony of the king in a letter addressed to the newspaper *Le Thermomètre*: "He climbed on the scaffold and went to the edge as if he wanted to speak to the crowd. But he was made to understand that this was now impossible. He let himself be led to the place where he was tied up and where he cried out loudly 'People, I die innocent'. Then, turning to us he told us: 'Gentlemen I am innocent of everything they accuse me of; I wish for my blood to cement the happiness of the French people.'" The scaffold was always surrounded by a double row of guards. On decapitation days, the square was overflowing with people. The crowd pushed and shoved in closely to see the show. To see better, they climbed on carts, they brought ladders, they gathered on terraces of the Tuileries, they climbed the trees on the Champs-Élysées. Those who rented lorgnettes were besieged. At the beginning of the "ceremony", the crowd was silenced. It was so they could hear the last words and the last shouts of the victims. Then came the deaf noise of the blade falling and that of the head rolling on the planks. Then the place came alive with cheers, shouts and howls when the executioner's assistant, obeying orders from the crowd, raised the bloody head of the victim. Calmly he strolled to each of the four corners of the dais so everyone had a chance to see it.

The Reign of Terror passed, the scaffold was pulled down. In 1799, the statue of Liberty was restored. "Liberty, liberty! what crimes have been commited in your name", had sighed Mme Roland while climbing the steps leading to the guillotine. A happy omen was found one day in the globe that the statue of Liberty held in its right hand. It was a nest of doves. The next year, the First Minister had it removed. The center of the square was empty. The obelisk of Luxor was given to Louis Philippe by the viceroy of Egypt, Méhemet-Ali, in October, 1838. Cleopatre's needle as Léon-Paul Fargue pleasantly calls it, "marks the center of the crossroads, on the very spot where the blood of a king was thrown like a bouquet from the summit of the old world".

During the Monarchy of July, Hittorff totally redesigned the square. On the small pavilions in each corner he placed eight statues that symbolize the cities of Brest, Rouen, Lyon, Marseille, Bordeaux, Nantes, Lille and Strasbourg and framed the obelisk with two monumental fountains that inspired Robert Desnos to write these lines a century later: *One beautiful day, the fountains suddenly sang to Paris, and the world was surprised, unaware that these nymphs of the Concorde held a captive king who cried.*

It was in 1852 that the ditches once used by girls as a pick-up place were filled in. The square is closed in, to the north, by two large symmetrical buildings made by Gabriel. The architecture reminds one of the colonnade of the Louvre. To the right of the Rue Royale is the Ministry of the Navy which was originally used to store the royal family's furniture. To the left is the Hôtel Crillon, one of the most prestigious hotels in Paris. Between these two buildings, the Rue Royale seems to be cut short at the Madeleine church.

In 1758, the Rue Royale was bordered by uniform buildings constructed from the plans of Jacques-Angel Gabriel, the architect who designed the Place de la Concorde. Burnt during the "Commune", the buildings on the street were immediately rebuilt exactly as they were and most of them are classified as Historical Monuments today.

It is especially since the end of the XIXth century that this has been a place for luxury. In 1910, the Marquis de Rochegude lamented that recently it had been "dishonored by so many commercial signs". Among them is that of the florist *Lachaume*, the oldest shop in the street, where you still can admire the floral displays in the shop windows, as well as the pastry shop *Ladurée*, whose macaroons have been the best in Paris for nearly a century. The restaurant *Maxim's* was established in 1891, by Gaillard Maxim. Employee of a bar situated at number 23 in the street, he bought the café Immoda, then on the verge of bankruptcy for having displayed a German flag in its window on July 14, 1890. The Universal Exhibition of 1900 was held largely near and around the Champs-Élysées and this attracted all the European aristocracy and its gracious as much as ruinous group of hangers-on. Since then the international *jet-set* as well as tourists have never ceased to frequent this temple of gastronomy whose Art Nouveau decor is extraordinarily intact.

The Concorde Bridge (pont de la Concorde) to the east of the square leads to the left bank. Begun in August, 1788, and finished in 1791, the engineer Perronet, who built it, used stones from the demolished Bastille prison for its construction. In this way Parisians could easily trample vestiges of royal tyranny.

Beyond the bridge, the colonnade of the National Assembly exactly faces the Madeleine church, which is situated at the other end of the Place de la Concorde. This façade dates only from 1807. It conceals a much older palace, built in 1728 for the Duchess of Bourbon, Louis XIV's legitimate daughter.

Acquired in 1784 by the Prince of Condé, the Palais-Bourbon was then enlarged by the addition of the hôtel de Lassay, which today is the residence of the president of the Assembly. Requisitioned by the Revolution, it held the Council of Five-Hundred, before being given back to Condé in 1815. The State acquired it definitively in 1827. The main hall, the hemicycle, was then redone to accommodate debates of the legislative body. It is today the seat of the National Assembly. When its members are in session the French flag is raised.

The Madeleine Church

It was in 1757 that it was decided to construct a church at the end of the all new Rue Royale. The architect Couture had already begun the project when the Revolution provisionally put an end to it. It was successively destined to be the Stock Exchange, the Trade Court, the Bank of France and even the Opera before Napoléon I, in 1806, decided that this monument would be a temple dedicated to the glory of the French armies. He chose the project by Vignon, who quickly tore down what had been erected

Cont. p. 89 ▶

63

Captions for photographs 30 to 53

30. The Louvre. The Pei pyramid. Another pyramid stood in front of the Louvre during the French Revolution. It was dedicated to the glory of Marat!

31. The fountains in the Napoléon courtyard of the Louvre.

32. Several sculptures in the Cour Marly (Richelieu wing).

33. The Jaconde (Mona Lisa) protected by glass from the crowds and fanatics.

34. The lights of Paris.

35. The Arc du Carrousel, built in 1806 by Napoléon I to celebrate the first victories of the Empire.

36. The Orsay station. This former train station, built in 1900 and closed since 1939, was happily turned into the Museum of XIXth Century Art.

37. A historic perspective from the Tuileries to La Défense, by way of the Concorde and the Champs-Élysées.

38. The Avenue de l'Observatoire, a continuation of the Luxembourg gardens. The fountain of the Observatoire, created by Davioud in 1873, combines the Chevaux Marins (sea horses) of Fremiet and symbols of the Four Corners of the World by Carpeaux.

39. The Palais-Royal. Between these two rows of columns designed by Fontaine in 1830 for Louis-Philippe, were the glass roof and sumptuous boutiques of one of the most beautiful arcades in Paris: The Gallery d'Orléans.

40. Under the arcades of the Palais-Royal there is only silence today. At the end of the XVIIIth century it was a hub-bub of gambling and prostitution which attracted all of Europe.

41. The Place Vendôme. Constructed by Mansard from 1687 to 1720. The column in the center was erected in 1810, replacing a statue of Louis XIV which was destroyed during the Revolution.

42. The entrance to the Hôtel Ritz. The most prestigious of all the grand hotels in Paris – pershaps in the world.

43. A detail of the Vendôme column. Built after the model of the Trajan column in Rome, it was made from melting 12,000 enemy canons taken after the Battle of Austerlitz.

44. The Garnier Opéra. Built by Charles Garnier during the Second Empire, opened in 1873, it is the masterpiece of Napoléon III style.

45. The Eiffel Tower and the Luxor obelisque illuminated. One is the most famous and the other the oldest monument in Paris.

46. The XIXth century glass dome of the Galeries Lafayette department store.

47. The Galerie Colbert, one of the most luxurious examples of these arcades which were in vogue in Paris between 1790 and 1840.

48. The Galerie du Lido. The oldest shopping gallery on the Champs-Élysées.

49. The Jouffroy arcades. Located on the Boulevard Montmartre, it houses the Musée Grévin, where those who make or have made history are represented by wax figures.

50. The façade of the National Assembly. Built in the XVIIIth century, the façade of this building and that of the Madeleine church are symmetrical. The façade hides the Bourbon Palace.

51. The end of a summer's day on the Champs-Élysées.

52. The Marly horses mark the entrance to the Champs-Élysées. These are only copies. The originals, works by Coustou, are in the Louvre, away from pollution. This one seems to be headed towards the Eiffel Tower.

53. The Arc of Triumph on the Place de l'Étoile at the end of the Champs-Élysées.

33

38

39

42

43

46

47

48

49

50

by Couture. In 1813, the Emperor, lacking finances, did an immediate about-face. "What will we do with a temple to Glory?", he declared. "Our grand ideas on that subject have changed. We need to give priests our temples to keep; they know how to conduct ceremonies and preserve a cult better than we do." The Temple of Glory was henceforth to become a church. Only in 1818 did the foundations begin to appear, and in 1824 the walls were only as high as the arches. It was in 1842 that the Madeleine church – in reality the Sainte Marie-Madeleine – was finally finished.

The Place de la Madeleine, whose construction was ordered in 1808 to frame the monument, has been open since 1824. Shops around the square are the gastronomic continuation of the luxury shops in the Rue Royale. Caterers and fine gourmet shops with legendary reputations offer their savory wares in beautiful window displays: *Fauchon*, *Hédiard*, the *Home of the Truffle* (la Maison de la Truffe). *Lucas-Carton*, one of the best restaurants in Paris, has kept its authentic 1900 decor with rich works in carved wood. The flower market that takes place every day gives this square a charm that somehow tempers the unceasing flow of traffic around it.

The Champs-Élysées

Just west of the Place de la Concorde, between two equestrian statues – the Horses of Marly (today only copies, the originals being in the Louvre, away from bad weather and pollution) – the Champs-Élysées stretches forth.
The Champs-Élysées was not always the prestigeous place that it has been for more than a century, neither were the gardens of this elegant promenade, where great restaurants and theatres are located.

It was in 1670 that Louis XIV conferred on Le Nôtre the task of making an elm-lined street in the marsh between the Tuileries and the present day Rond-Point, with lawns and gardens on either side. In 1710, the street was prolonged to the top of the hill where the Arc of Triumph is located today. A bridge was built over the large sewer that crossed the Rond-Point before it emptied into the waters of the Seine. The Champs-Élysées, which was outside Paris at that time, did not have a very good reputation. "One night the police surprised an abbot who was in a very compromising position with a black girl." Police reports of the period note that "The abbot was not prosecuted on condition that he would no longer hear confessions at night under the trees". This ill-famed place had a great number of underground caves and tunnels where all sorts of delinquents lived. The rare shacks and dance halls did not draw large crowds. The street ended in vacant lots and pastures.
Strangely, it was during the Revolution that crowds began to frequent the avenue... and more particularly from the time the guillotine was set up on the Place de la Révolution. People came with friends and in large numbers to see heads roll! They came there to howl, shout and abuse the victims. They sometimes came there to die with a loved one. It was a multicolored and mixed crowd of bloodthirsty revolutionaries, hysterical knitters, fervent republicans, who came to have a little fun. And then, once Sanson, the executioner, had shown them several severed heads, the whole crowd went merrily on their way to talk about the behevior of each victim. They went to one of the dance halls on the "Champs". Among these modest smoky bars was one surrounded by a terrace and rented by the citizen Doyen. Modified some years later, it would become the famous Ledoyen restaurant.
The Directoire filled in the caves and tun-

nels at the same time that the central part of the street was widened. In 1800, only six houses, situated at the far end, on the hill, flanked the street.

In 1815, Russian and English troops that had conquered Napoléon, camped there, at the very gates to Paris. The trunks of the century-old elms were destroyed by their horses and the lawns and gardens disappeared. After being ruined, the Champs-Élysées was again out of favor with Parisians despite attempts at restoration. In 1836, the architect Horeau described the avenue like this: "Each season brings problems. In winter it is the mud, in summer the dust. In any season, after the slightest shower, the ditches fill with muddy water that pollutes the very air and causes thousands of accidents. Under trees and in the cellars there is revolting filthiness. Everyone knows that at night this place is the shameful refuge for men and women of ill-repute as well as a haven for criminals." In 1833, Louis- Philippe ordered Hittorff to renovate the Champs-Élysées. He paved the avenue and redesigned the gardens. He tidied up the shrubs, drew geometrical plans for the sides of the Concorde and built four fountains in the same style, which were dedicated to Venus, Diana, the Four Seasons, and to the "Élysée". Nevertheless, he kept the immense water jet that, since 1817, has gushed in the middle of the Rond-Point. The new gardens were illuminated by wrought iron candelabrums! It was due to his initiative that numerous luxury restaurants and cafés opened there: *Ledoyen, Laurent, the Ambassadors* (today the *Espace Cardin*). A circus set up its tent there (the *Summer Circus,* under the Second Empire called the *Empress' Circus*), that could seat more than six thousand people. There the famous Franconi performed and, later, the beautiful Otéro. A Panorama opened onto the square Marigny. All of this helped to launch the Champs-Élysées.

In 1855 the first French Universal Exhibition took place in the Palace of Industry, an immense building made of glass and iron. It had been built in the gardens of the Champs-Élysées especially for the occasion. All the crowned heads of Europe, princes, financiers and tycoons of industry thronged the Avenue that became one of the most elegant places of Paris.

The Palace of Industry, judged too small to hold the new Exhibition in 1900, was demolished. It was on this occasion that the Grand Palace and the Petit Palace were constructed. Built in record time from 1897 to 1900, the Grand Palace would house the Museum of Fine Arts. It opened its doors with two shows: a restrospective exhibition of Fine Arts and *the Centennale* that confirmed the success of the Impressionists. It continued with all the great shows and exhibitions connected with the plastic arts: The French Artists' Show, the Autumn Exhibition, where Fauves in 1905, Gauguin in 1906 and Cézanne in 1907 triumphed successively.

The Independants' Show was devoted to the cubists and their leader, Picasso. In the Palace of Fine Arts, the rooms have since been used for exhibitions such as the Book Fair, antique shows and the FIAC. On the north side of the building, great temporary painting exhibitions are held. Destined for the grand retrospective of French Art during the Universal Exhibition, the Petit Palace was built on the site of the Palace of Industry, by Charles Girault. Since its inauguration, May 1, 1900, it has housed artistic collections of the city of Paris. Similar to the temporary exhibitions that are shown there, we can admire major works of the painter Courbet. There is a hall devoted to Odilon Redon and a remarkable series of works by the painter Nabis. Between the Grand Palace and the Petit Palace, the avenue is as large as the Champs-Élysées. In keeping with this monumental splendor is the ornamental richness of the bridge

Alexandre III which, since 1900, has offered a spectacular perspective that connects the Invalides to the Champs-Élysées.

A long-time symbol of the prestige and luxury of Paris, the Avenue des Champs-Élysées has, since the 70's, lost some of its luster. Sophisticates, little by little, have deserted it. Princes and their entourages have disappeared. Its buildings, from the end of the century up to the year 1930, were destroyed and replaced slowly by office buildings, financial groups and insurance companies. Only those of the Païva and the Duke of Morny still stand. The first, whose interior decoration is a sumptuous example of the Second Empire Parisian style has become the seat of the Travellers Club, the second that of the Marcel Dassault group, which makes military aircraft.

The rare exceptions are Guerlain, which has preserved its elegant façade in wrought iron, commissioned by Jacques Guerlain in 1914, from the architect Mewes; and Mercedes, which reminds us that in the 1930's, all the prestigeous automobile manufacturers had showrooms on the "Champs".

As for the Avenue Montaigne, the Rue du Faubourg Saint-Honoré, the Rue François Ier... neons have covered façades in the Broadway style. The great residences that attracted fortunes from the whole world have faded away. The Claridge, transformed into a hotel, is the only one left. But the Astoria and the Élysée Palace have long since disappeared. Stalls of sale goods are on display among itinerants and street musicians. The *fast-food* restaurants, which reek of greasy French fries have, little by little, replaced the cafés and restaurants that once made this avenue so charming. Of these bygone days only *Fouquet's* remains. In 1901 Léopold Mourier bought a small café at the corner of the Champs-Élysées and the present-day Avenue George V, the proprietor of which was Mr Fouquet. Following the example of Maxim's he anglicized its name. Soon after, race horse owners and *gentlemen riders* met there often. Some years later, the cinema crowd took over, following the French actor Raimu. Soon, Gabin, Belmondo, and others succeeded him. Today, it is at *Fouquet's* that *the night of the Césars* (the French movie awards) finishes, after the best films of the year have received their rewards. Fargue said of this restaurant that it was "a place for men to gossip". Then he added, "One of those places that cannot do without people, unless there is a bombing, and even then! It is an indispensable organ for the good health of Paris. Fouquet's is like the National Library of the Parisian sophisticate". All that still remains for it is to be classified a Historical Monument!

Despite the recent renovation that, happily, has given the sidewalks back to pedestrians, the unceasing flow of traffic that invades the Champs-Élysées, has made it one of the most polluted places in Paris. Nevertheless, to all these negatives, defenders of the Champs-Élysées reply that cries of alarm announcing the decline of the Champs-Élysées are not new... and do not keep the avenue from attracting crowds. Already in 1917, "Friends of the Champs-Élysées, such as Gaston Louis Vuitton, wanted a double row of tidy trees and the sidewalks left to strollers".

If shops are no longer what they were, they nevertheless make more money than ever. People go there to buy things at a cheaper price. This could be, after all, just a sign of the times! Shops cater to their clientele: office workers of the quarter and tourists that pour out of buses daily. And the dream remains; it is good for merchants, when their businesses prosper, to have a shop on the most famous avenue in the world!

The Place de l'Étoile

Situated on a former hill, the Place de l'Étoile was leveled in 1774. The rise was lowered five meters, and the earth thus recuperated shored up the Champs-Élysées and formed the slopes of the current Rue Balzac and Rue Washington. In 1787, Ledoux placed two heavy monuments there, between the Rue Tilsitt and the Rue Presbourg, that formed a customs house for the gate into Paris.

Construction of the Arc of Triumph began only in 1806. By a decree of February 18, of that year, Napoléon, on his return from Austerlitz, ordered it built. Chalgrin began the work. But his death in 1811 left the Arc unfinished. Work started again only twelve years later. In 1831, only the masonry was finished. Louis-Philippe became king and was hated by the republicans, who reproached him for "having stolen the revolution of 1830, their revolution". Monarchists never forgave him for being the son of Philippe Equality, this Duke d'Orléans who had voted for the death of his cousin Louis XVI. To rally bonapartists, still a very active party, the king once again undertook Chalgrin's project to continue the legend of the *little corporal*.

In 1836, names of battles and six hundred generals of the empire were engraved on the monument. But that of General Hugo, the father of the poet, was forgotten. The general had nevertheless been a member of the army of the Rhine before going to Vendée in 1792 and 1793. He had rallied the army of Italy in 1805, then had followed Joseph Bonaparte, King of Spain, to Madrid in 1808. Having become his aide de camp, he had saved the king's life during the retreat at Vittoria in 1813. This omission inspired Victor Hugo to write this poem on the Arc de Triomphe:

Oh! vast monument, chiseled by history,
Heap of stone sitting on a heap of glory.
I regret nothing before your sublime wall, except
the absence of Phidias, and my father forgotten...

In 1836, Louis-Philippe came in person to inaugurate the Arc. Thirty years had passed since August 15, 1806, when Napoléon had placed the first stone. It is the largest and tallest arc ever built in the world. Its volume is twenty times superior to that of Severe Septime in Rome, and its weight (fifty thousand tons) seven times superior to that of the Eiffel Tower. For all that, it is not finished. Different projects were proposed to crown its summit: a chariot drawn by six horses, an effigy of the Emperor on a heap of arms, a large star, a crown, a gigantic eagle or even an apotheosis of Napoléon on a terrestrial globe. At the burial of Victor Hugo, a plaque designed by Falguière was installed provisionally... and remained several years, before being pulled down, as it was damaged by the weather.

On January 28, 1921, to perpetuate the memory of soldiers fallen during World War I, an anonymous soldier who died at Verdun, the Unknown Soldier, was buried under the Arc of Triumph. Until that time, cars, carriages and buses had the right to pass under the arch. Traffic crossed the square in all directions and accidents were frequent.

The area around the Arc is adorned by buildings designed by Hittorff under the Second Empire. The Baron Haussmann, finding them disappointing, too low as compared to the Arc, asked that they be hidden behind trees. They were called "Hotels of the Marshals" in harmony with neighbouring avenues which bear the names of marshals of the Empire. The Rue de Presbourg and the Rue de Tilsitt that circle the square, follow the former layout of patrol paths from the time when it was still a gate to the city of Paris.

Around the Champs-Élysées

A part of the luxury lost by the Champs-Élysées is found in neighbouring streets. South of the avenue is what one calls today the Golden Triangle. The sides of this triangle? The Avenue Montaigne, the Avenue George V and the part of the Champs from the Rond-Point to the metro station George V. Crossed in the middle by the Rue François I, this triangle encloses the greatest concentration of luxury business in Paris. The most prestigious labels such as Yves St Laurent, Givenchy, Nina Ricci, Chanel, Christian Dior, Bulgari, Cartier, Vuitton, as the head offices of principal radio stations, RTL and Europe 1; public and private television channels: France 2, France 3, and M6, and multinational companies are located there.

On the other side of the Rond-Point of the Champs-Élysées, in the continuation of the Avenue Montaigne, comes the Avenue Matignon. There, within a hundred or so meters, spreads the private domain of the great Parisian art galleries: Artcurial, Findlay, Étienne Sassi, Didier Imbert Fine Art, the Gallery Maeght, Tamenaga and the gallery Maurice Garnier, that is devoted exclusively to Bernard Buffet. This avenue is soon cut by the Rue du Faubourg Saint-Honoré, another great artery for Paris luxury. Art galleries continue, but also famous antique dealers, that show off their treasures. Perrin, Steinitz, Cailleux, Aaron and everyone who is anyone in luxury ready-to-wear: Hermès, Yves St Laurent, Lanvin, Versace, Lacroix, Cardin, or those undisputed temples of beauty, such as Carita and the Institute St Laurent, whose decorator, Jacques Grange, made the beauty shop unequalled in its refinement. All external signs of Parisian elegance are on display in the shop windows of this Rue du Faubourg Saint-Honoré, where the only austere and mysterious intruder is the Élysée Palace – The Palace of the Republic. Becoming the Rue Saint-Honoré after crossing the Rue Royale (where in the XVIIIth century one of the principal gates to Paris was located), it ends a bit farther on at the Rue Castiglione and the Place Vendôme.

The Élysée

The Élysée Palace was built in 1718 by the Count of Évreux. Upon his death in 1753, the Évreux Mansion was awarded to Madame de Pompadour. Louis XV inherited it upon the death of the Marchioness. He used it as a warehouse for the furnishings he would use to decorate the structure being built for him on the Place de la Concorde by Gabriel.

Then it passed successively between the hands of the banker Beaujon, Louis XVI, then on to duchess of Bourbon-Condé who fitted in its park a hamlet of the pastoral type in the style of the Trianon. When in 1794 the duchess fled the country, the palace was sequestrated under the Revolution. It was sold in 1798 to Monsieur Hovyn who, under the name of Hamlet of Chantilly, transformed it into an amusement park with a rollor-coaster, balls and other merrymaking. His daughter installed shops in the Hamlet and divided buildings into apartments which she rented. In one of them, M. and Mme de Vigny moved in with their young son, Alfred. The poet evokes this stay in his *Mémoires*: "In the silence of the great apartments and these beautiful gardens whose gates opened up to the Champs-Élysées, I received my first education. There was my native atmosphere, and there my studies and my gymnasium."

In 1805 the palace was bought by Napoléon, who gave it as a gift to his sister, Caroline Murat. After the Murats departed for Naples in 1808, Napoléon planned to turn it into a residence for his son – but finally it was given to Joséphine as a "divorce gift".

It was at the Élysée that, in 1815, Napoléon signed his second abdication with the Emperor of Russia and Wellington, who lived there then.

Changing proprietors several times again, the palace was in turn the residence for a host of notables – the Bey of Tunis and the Queen of Spain resided there – it was the property of Queen Amélie, the wife of Louis-Philippe, before becoming in 1848, the residence of Prince Louis-Napoléon Bonaparte after his election to the presidency of the Republic. It was from there that he directed his coup d'état of December 2, 1851, that was to lead France into the Second Empire.

After his defeat in the Sudan, in 1817, and the proclamation of the Third Republic, the Élysée returned to its function of being the residence of the President. And if Adolphe Thiers never resided there, MacMahon, his successor, established himself there in 1874, inaugurating a long tradition that was followed by the twenty presidents that succeeded him, right on up until the present day.

The Place Vendôme

This site is without dispute one of the architectural ornaments of Paris, with its natural continuation from the Rue de la Paix, opened by Napoléon I in 1806. Recently renovated by the city, the Place Vendôme lets us admire the layout of its noble façades, the work of Jules Mansart. For Georges Cain, the street and the square at the beginning of the century formed "the promised land of elegance, where woven gold dresses and money flourished; where fabulous coats were lavishly embroidered; where flowered hats were as much works of art as those of a silversmith, and plumes like those of Louis XIV's knights; charming young girls with painted nails, all graceful and pretty, were the models, the sales ladies and the errant girls of well-known milliners or great dressmakers with legendary names: Reboux, Virot, Doucet, Paquin, etc.".

In our days, on the ground floor of the splendid XVIIth century buildings that make up the square, common jewelers have been replaced by the greats of fashion: *Van Cleff and Arpels*, *Boucheron*, *Chaumet*, *Cartier*, now occupy these arcade shops. *The Hotel Ritz* is located at number 19 and has, since it came into existence, participated in the prestige of the square. Its founder, César Ritz, explained to its architect: "I want it hygienic, comfortable, beautiful, and, above all, totally and perfectly elegant." From its opening, in 1898, each apartment, had its own bathroom then an unusual luxury, and was outfitted with a telephone.

The Ministry of Justice occupies numbers 11 and 13, logically taking the location of the former Chancery of the Kingdom.

At number 12, Chopin died on October 17, 1849. Two days previously, after suffering a crisis, he saw at his bedside the Countess Delphine Potocka. In a weak voice, he begged her to sing. Everyone believed him to be delirious. Even so, he continued insisting. Then, recounted Franz Lizt, a piano was brought into his bedroom and the countess "grand, slender, dressed in white", eyes drowned with tears, sang an air of *Stradella* and a psalm by *Marcello*. Those in attendance, filled with emotion, knelt while the superb voice cradled the invalid. "It was nightfall. Chopin's sister, overcome near the bed, could no longer bear up."

The Place Vendôme was built between 1687 and 1720, on the site of the mansion of the son of Henri IV and Gabrielle d'Estrées: Alexandre, Duke of Vendôme. In 1699, an equestrian statue of Louis XIV, the work of Girardon, dominated the center. It was destroyed during the Revolution in September, 1792, like so many other shameful symbols of the royal domination. Celebrated throughout all Europe, this statue served as a model to Peter the Great who, in St Petersburg, was still at the Neva.

The column that replaced it was raised in 1810. Forty-four meters high and built on the model of the Trajan column in Rome, it was fabricated from melted enemy bronze canons captured in the Battle of Austerlitz. Its true name is the *Austerlitz Column* or the *Grand Army Column*. It celebrates the exploits of the Napoleonic troops. A statue of the Emperor is installed at the summit. "Oh Napoléon, at all hours in his waistcoat and laurel", mused Colette, over a century later, learning on her elbows at the very top of the square.

In May, 1871, some Commune members destroyed the column, following the desires of the painter Courbet who dreamed of smelting the bronze of the column with that of the Krupp canons, victors in the Sudan, so as to erect in its place "The column of Germany and France forever in solidarity". The column was decreed a "monument of barbarity, a symbol of brute force and false glory", and it was decided that it be destroyed.

On May 16, 1871, standing on the balcony of the current Ministry of Justice, in the presence of eminent members of the Commune, the painter attended the ceremony of the column's devastation. The historian Lissaray, an eye witness, said, "When the head of Bonaparte rolled on the ground, an immense acclamation poured forth, like people freed, from thousands of chests. People played in the ruins and cheered enthusiastically, the red flag flying on this purified pedestral that became that day *the altar of the human species.*

The celebration lasted a long time! People from Versailles having taken over Paris, all the Commune members believed it exemplary to be photographed in front of the collapsed column with their weapons. As for Courbet, he was condemned to pay the expense of rebuilding of the Column, which was 323,091,068 francs. Legend has it that he had to paint the rest of his days – he died six years later – to pay his debt. But he himself confided to one of his friends in 1872, "If the Commune was the source of my displeasure, it only caused the sales (of my paintings) to go up by fifty per cent. In that case, just let the masses rave on".

The Garnier Opera

The Garnier Opera is without question the best example of the architectural splendor of the Second Empire. Recognized as the most immense of antiquated opera houses (eleven thousand square meters), everything there is excessive. The Great Foyer measures fifty-four meters long and on stage, close to five hundred persons can easily perform. As for the auditorium, it can accommodate up to two thousand two-hundred spectators. The chandelier that illuminates it weighs six tons! It came crashing down one evening in 1896 without too much damage.

When the Empress Eugénie saw the Opera for the first time, she was overwhelmed at such an abundance of marble, colorful paintings, gold, onyx and purple crystal, with such excessive decorative flourishes, such a profusion of winged spirits, nude nymphs, fountains and columns. As the architect Charles Garnier was at her side, she asked him enchantedly, "Sir, what style is this?" "It is in the Napoléon III mode," he replied.

"The new Opera has just opened and to appearances, it is a prosperous one", wrote Henry James in his *Parisian Sketches.* "It has been, at any moment of these last six years, the most viewed architectural phenomenon of Paris. This Opera is already a historical monument; it summarizes in a sensitive and visible form what the Empire planned to be, and it constitutes a sort of emblem – a very favorable emblem – of what the Empire means to France. Opinions can diverge about the beauty of the building. In my opinion, it is not beautiful; but nobody can deny that it is superbly singular; that it reflects its period, that it tells the history of the society that produced it. If that, as some people believe, is the first duty of a great structure, the Opera is an incomparable success."

The first stone was put into place in 1862, but an underground water table slowed the construction for some time. At the fall of the Empire (1870) the work was interrupted. During the Commune (1871), its vast rooms served as a prison and as warehouses.

It was inaugurated on January 5, 1875, in the presence of the President of the Republic, MacMahon. This was a significant event in Parisian life as reported by Charles Simond in his *Echoes of Paris* in the year 1875. "By early morning, several hundred people surrounded the structure; by afternoon the crowd increased hour by hour. That night by curtain time, and in the evening, at the moment of entry, one could reckon at least seven or eight thousand the number of the curious who crowded around the Place de l'Opéra, on its adjacent boulevards and in the neighbouring streets. Inside the orchestra seats were almost empty until eight o'clock. By seating oneself before the moment when the hall would become filled, one could take in all that was going on.

The curtain was a splendid red, with a large gold fringe, and framed the prosecnium spectacularly. The light of the chandelier was ample; the light from its upper sections reflected the clear rose color of the dome. The effect in general is excellent. This hall is truly magnificent... One comes mainly to admire it!"

Charles Garnier, its architect, former protégé of Napoléon III, was not invited to its inauguration. He went there nevertheless, but only by paying for his orchestra seat! Since the opening of the Opera at Bastille, the Garnier Opera is in principal entirely devoted to dance. Management and organization problems do not prevent it from continuing to have performances! (It seems that this radical separation of ballet from opera is becoming more pronounced).

The Garnier Opera operates a museum, founded in 1868, that occupies the Rotunda, initially anticipated for Napoléon III. Many artists' souvenirs, busts and portraits, instruments and accessories, scenery and costumes, posters and programs evoke the history of the Opera – as well as *The Opera Fire on the Rue Le Peletier in* 1871 by Hubert Robert. The library, recently reopened, contains close to a hundred thousand works retracing its choreographic and musical history, as well as all scores played at the Paris Opera since 1669.

Montmartre

In 1860 Napoléon III, by the new boundries that he drew, doubled the area of Paris by annexing villages on the periphery. It is how many churches became Parisian, including those of Auteuil, Passy, Batignolles, Belleville, Monceau... and Montmartre.

Several years previously, Nerval wrote: "There are mills, cabarets and arbours, rustic fields and silent lanes, with cottages, barns and bushy gardens; steep plains, where springs flow, forming greenery and islets where goats graze and eat the brush hanging on the boulders. There are even vineyards. The last vintage celebrates Montmartre, which, in Roman times, battled with Argenteuil and Suresnes." The mills on the hill have today disappeared, and with them the bushy gardens as well. There no longer remains a cottage or a barn, and the springs are dry. The charm lingers nevertheless, despite houses which are often too tidy and too scrubbed, and that give the top of the hill the look of a movie set. But isn't tourism a sort of theatre that plays a role in the city? And this tourism represents more than 60% of the commercial activity of Montmartre.

The origin of Montmartre goes back to ancient times. A well-established legend from the Vth century says that St Denis was beheaded there, along with two of his companions, for not having renounced their God. After the severence, the Saint, carrying his head between his hands, went to wash in a spring (at the impass Girardon, dry since the XIXth century), before returning to the village on foot. The village was baptized Saint-Denis later. The hill then became "Mount of martyrs" and later, by contraction, Montmartre.

Since then the place has remained one of the sacred places for Christianity. Thus in the XIIth century the church Saint-Pierre-de-Montmartre was built there, on the site of a very ancient sanctuary dedicated to St Denis. This small church was consecrated by Pope Eugene III on Easter Monday, 1147. Built in the Gothic style, it is among the oldest churches in Paris. Its modern stained glass windows in bright colors were given by an anonymous donor in 1950. In the adjoining cemetery no one has been buried since 1858. This disorderly desertion is in sharp contrast to the neat appearance of the Place du Tertre, which is just nearby.

Much more famous and just as religious is the Sacré-Cœur. After the Commune, in a period when it was feared that religious sentiment was dangerously on the decline in France, the idea to raise a basilica on the site of an ancient abbey devoted to the cult of the Sacré-Cœur (Sacred Heart) was born. An incredible national vigor mobilized in its favor. The Nationaly Assembly ordered its construction in the public interest. A national subscription followed, bringing gifts and offerings from all over France. Begun in 1876, work finished only in 1919. The subsoil posed huge problems, underground waters having transformed the hill into a dangerous and gigantic honeycomb, where tunnels and underground galleries ran together.

Paris is now used to this "huge meringue" protector. Its luminous white color is due to the surprising stone chosen for its construction. The stone comes from quarries in the Loiret and does not get dull with age. The architect P. Abadie insisted that stone alone be used in the construction, excluding all use of wood or metal supports. The Sacré-Cœur is part of the Parisian skyline, the same as the Eiffel Tower or the Arc de Triomphe. One gets there by wide steps that lead to a porch whose beautiful bronze doors, sculpted with scenes from the Gospel, are the work of Hippolyte Lefèvre. One of them represents *the Devotion of France to the Sacred Heart*. The interior is a strange "neo-romano-byzantin" style. The murals are made up exclusively of mosaics, whose gold shines in the dim light of candles.

One climbs the hill to visit the Sacré-Cœur and discover the place du Tertre, with its painters and its poets. Then, as the stroll continues, one gladly loses oneself in the nearby streets: the calm Rue Cortot, the Rue Saint-Rustic, the oldest on the hill; the Rue des Saules that leads to the vineyard and to the *Lapin Agile*. Everywhere one can explore the sudden staircases that Mouloudji sings about and which are exhausting to the local inhabitants. At the top there is an exceptional panorama of the city to discover.

Once past the Sacré-Cœur and the church of Saint-Pierre, the *place du Tertre* opens to the large overflow of tourists. The houses that surround this square are authentic houses of past centuries. (It is good to underline this, especially here, where you can doubt everything.) The houses protect the painters from the wind. In this square painters churn out stereotyped images of a Montmartre that has disappeared. Their "brothers", the caricaturists, can be seen just as well in Rome, London or Hamburg.

Then the Rue Norvins opens between art galleries and souvenir shops. Farther on, an old whim of the XVIIIth century, the *Folie Sandrin*, bears out its name better than in the past century. One Doctor Blanche opened a clinic for lunatics there. Nerval lived there for eight months. He recorded his impressions in *Promenades and Memories*: "What enchanted me above all in this small space, sheltered by the large trees of the château des Brouillards, is that the vineyard is all that remains linked to the memory of Saint-Denis. After that is the vicinity of the old watering hole for the animals, where horses and dogs are bathed. The fountain, built in the old style is where those who come there to wash would chat and sing as in the first chapter of 'Werther.'"

The vineyard has remained intact and is lovingly protected just a few steps away from the Folie Sandrin. Each harvest is a time for merrymaking. For sure the wine is not good, but to see Paris while harvesting grapes on the hill is a privilege! It takes place on the anniversary of the "Free Commune of Montmartre". Little children (called Poulbots) and cooks parade through the streets, all dressed in red, white and blue. The Mayor is on hand and the head of the police, dressed in a superb Second Empire uniform. On this occasion a race takes place among the café waiters. They wear their aprons and carry loaded trays at arm's length. The race is all the more perilous as they run through steep streets and up and down stairways on the hill.
Opposite the vineyard is le *Lapin Agile* (the agile rabbit). This former inn was one of the favorites of Bohemian Montmartre. In the smoke, in the midst of canvasas donated by patrons, then neither rich nor famous, Max Jacob, Utrillo, Dorgelès, Carco, Mac Orlan, Charles Dullin, Picasso, Verlaine and even Courteline came to drink and prolong the night. Sometimes there were fearsome fights, when low life, hoodlums and girls from the Caulaincourt quarter or the Rue Lamark came there to "settle their accounts".

Victor, the son of the owner "Frédé" was killed in the course of one of these wicked evenings. Those who dreamed of poetry and painting soon fled to other cafés.
Today there are shows, with drinks, that continue the tradition of these evenings where, in the 1950's, young unknows came to make their debuts. They had names like: Georges Brassens, Claude Nougaro, Alexandre Lagoya...

On the hillside opposite, on the other side of the Place Jean-Baptiste Clément, the slope leads to the Rue Girardon and the Rue Lepic. There you can see the last two mills of Montmartre. There were about thirty or so in the XVIIIth century! But *Blute-fin* and *le Radet* are now only make-believe. It has been a long time since the wind whistled in their still and silent sails. At least they evoke a bucolic past, the time *Where thirty windmills, blades extended, teach me each day that the wind chases the clouds away.* (Régnard)
The folk singers Béranger, Bruant and so many others have continued to praise these windmills, where on celebration days, hung ribbons and bonnets of the prettiest young girls.
Blute-fin the larger of the two surviving windmills, dominates the neighbouring garden of the large hall of the *Moulin de la Galette*. It has its legend. On March 30, 1814, while enemies of Napoléon I besieged Paris, a battery of nine canons had been installed on Montmartre. When the Prussians came up the hill, soldiers were massacred, without ever abandoning their positions. Among the soldiers killed were three of the four Debray brothers, the sons of the *Blute-fin's* owner. After the cease-fire order was given, the eldest of the Debray brothers, bound to avenge his borthers, refused to surrender and fired buckshot on an advancing Russian column... A bayonnet nailed him to the door of the mill. In the last instant of his life, he killed the commanding officer of the detachment with a bullet

from his pistol. His body was immediately carved into four pieces, each attached to one of the blades of his windmill.

His son, who escaped, became a miller himself, following in the footsteps of his father. Although he was a hard worker, he had, nevertheless, one weakness: dancing. As soon as his day's work was done, his pleasure was to teach the youth of Montmartre the secrets of acrobatic dancing. His free lessons were a vivid success... and became paying, when the miller started making a big deal of them. Thus was created the public ballroom *Le Moulin de la Galette* (The Mill of the cake). Between dances, in the shade of the garden, Debray served warm cake sprinkled with a small glass of the local wine.

This fashion became quite popular. All of the artistic community became regulars of the Mill. "Beside this mill... where all the pretty Parisian girls are, already tainted by vice, they drink white wine with gentlemen of the street, under the large immobile blades, in the shadow of Sacré-Cœur – which seems to ask the sky for a little indulgence for the sinners of the Mill", wrote Deschaumes. Van Gogh, Utrillo, Corot and many others would immortalize this famous ballroom that inspired Renoir to paint one of his more famous canvases. The mill *Le Radet*, more modest, decorated a little garden next to the ballroom.

A bit farther, on the Place Emile Goudeau, the *Bateau-Lavoir* can be found. Following the fire of May, 1970, its façade and entry were reconstructed like the original. Built partly in wood, its initial name was "Home of the Trapper" until Max Jacob critized this famous landmark because of the washing that was always hanging in its windows. Among its tenants, listed out of order: Picasso, who painted the *Demoiselles of Avignon* there, Van Dongen, Braque, Matisse, Degas, Derain, Poulbot, Modigliani, Suzanne Valadon and her son Utrillo, cantor of Montmartre if ever there

was one. Van Gogh and Corot were also tenants there. Impressionists, cubists and "fauves" worked together in workshops and studios of this modest cottage to reinvent painting. Poets also came in numbers to work there, such as Apollinaire, Mac Orlan, Max Jacob, Dorgelès, Gertrude Stein... and Paul Doumer who much later became President of the Republic. Being Bohemian there, at that time, led to just about anything.

Montmartre life was not limited to the hill itself, although today it constitutes the main appeal. The Boulevard Clichy and the immediate surroundings of Montmartre are also full and rich with history. The Bohemians held out there until the beginning of the century, and night clubs, cafés and studios were everywhere. Today many artists still live there, in the middle of the sex-shops that have replaced cinemas and cafés. At number 6 of the Boulevard Clichy, Degas spent the last years of his life. He died in 1917 in his studio on the 5th floor, in the middle of his collection of paintings that brought together works of El Greco, Gauguin, Daumier, Delacroix, Ingres and Cézanne. In this same building the American Mary Cassatt lived and worked. She was a friend and protégée of Degas. Later Matisse would work for some time in the studio on the top floor that the painter Michel Rémy-Bieth occupies today. On the opposite sidewalk are the high glass windows of Crhisto's workshop. He is the artist who wrapped up the Pont-Neuf. At number 11 Boulevard Clichy, the actress Sarah Bernhardt, sculptor in her time, rented a workshop from 1873, her apartment in the Rue de Rome being too small for her to make her models properly. She spent mornings there, days even, when she was free from rehearsals. In 1909, Picasso, 28 years old then, was a tenant there for a time. Daumier, another painter and caricaturist, lived a long time at number 36. Until his death in 1904, Gérome lived at number 65. Music should

Cont. p. 121 ▶

Captions for photographs
54 to 72

54. The Moulin Rouge in the Place Blanche. Its famous show was founded in 1889.

55. The church of Sacré-Cœur. Begun in 1876, the construction lasted forty years.

56. On the "Butte" (hill). In the background can be seen the church of Saint-Pierre which partly hides Sacré-Cœur.

57. Painters give folklore to the Place du Tertre.

58. Sacré-Cœur watches over Paris.

59. The Pont Alexandre III (1900). Built at the same time as the Petit Palais and the Grand Palais, this bridge symbolizes the Franco–Russian alliance of 1896. In the middle are two large copper shields representing a nymph of the Seine and the other a nymph of the Neva.

60. The Invalides seen from the esplanade side. In the foreground, the "barracks" (1671), and above, the dome of the church by J.H. Mansart (1706).

61. The old soldier on the Alma bridge keeps an eye on the level of the Seine. During the great flood of 1910 the water level was up to his shoulders... usually he is high and dry on his pedestal.

62. The Pont Mirabeau, full of memories of Apollinaire and Marie Laurencin's love affair, in front of the new high rises along the Seine. A strange contrast!

63. The Eiffel tower seen from the Alexandre III bridge.

64. July 14th, at night.

65. The Rodin Museum.

66. Bewilderment or admiration?

67. Three women by Maillol in the Tuileries gardens.

68. The Arche de La Défense.

69. A Calder mobile in front of office blocks in La Défense.

70. The Arche de La Défense and its permanent "cloud". Its architect wanted it to be an "Arch to the Triumph of Man".

71. The esplanade of La Défense framed by the high rise office blocks of multinational companies.

72. The Bagatelle rose garden in the bois de Boulogne.

55

56

57

58

61

62

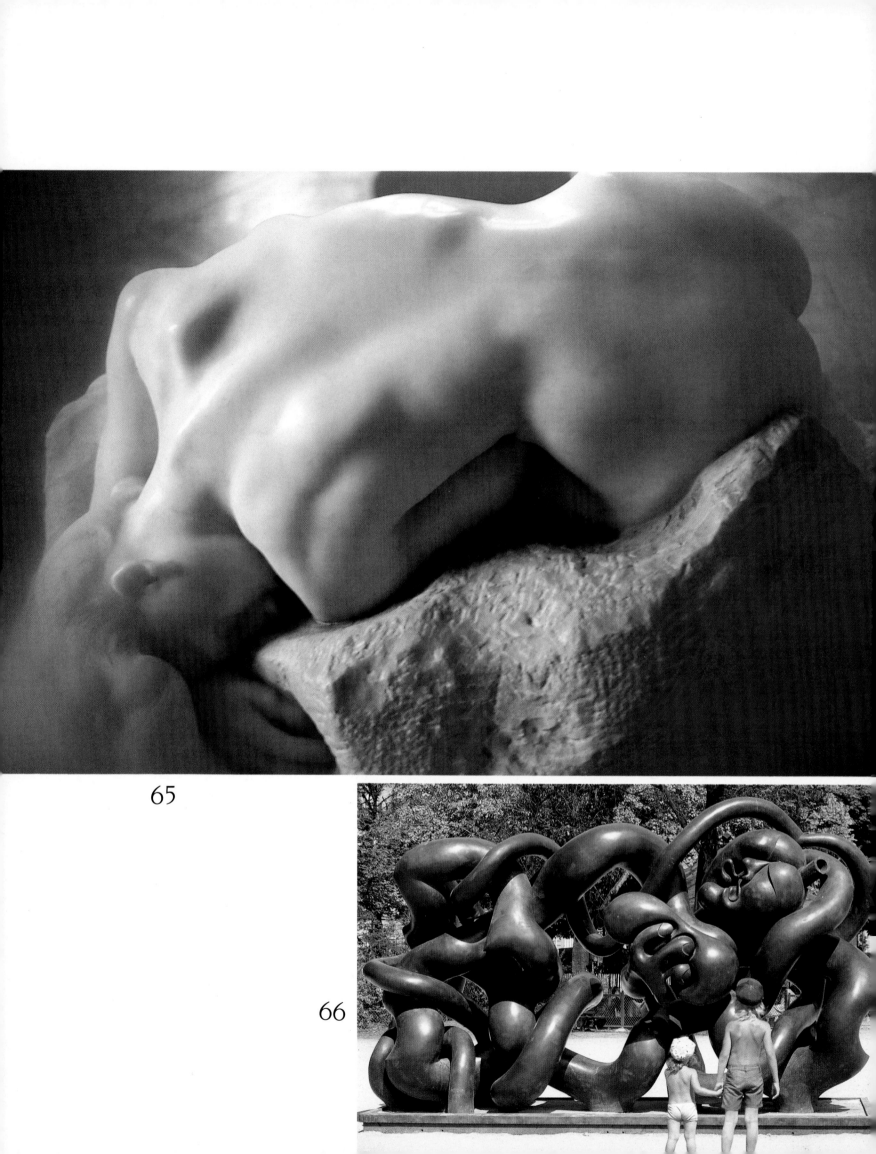

65

66

not be left out. Darius Milhaud lived at number 10, Henri Sauguet at number 41 and Honegger at number 71. Berlioz died in the Rue de Calais. The café *Cyrano* in the Place Blanche became the rendez-vous of surrealists when Breton resided in the Rue Fontaine. The entire area was that of the Bohemians – their domaine. Those who lived above, those who lived below made the theatres and cabarets of Montmatre a success. The *Caveau du Chat Noir*, founded in 1881, was where Alphonse Allais gave his classes. Steinlen advertised it with his many posters. The *Moulin Rouge*, the most famous of all, opened on May 1, 1889, to amuse the throngs of visitors to the Universal Exhibition. Both an open air theatre and a music hall, it was almost immediately an extraordinary success. High society gladly came there to have fun. Toulouse-Lautrec would immortalize its artists and performers, such as Goulue, Jeanne Avril and Valentin le Désossé, as well as the night-owls that hung out there. It is at the Moulin Rouge that the Four Arts annual ball was held (Quat'z Arts). This famous celebration, a masked ball, brought together, with traditional din, pupils and teachers of all painting, sculpture, engraving and architecture schools in town.

The *Cigale Music Hall*, created in 1880, has found its youth again by hosting stars of the *show business* world of today.

The cinema is also important and not to be forgotten, even if it no longer flourishes in this quarter that counted, fifty years ago, close to 70 theatres. Let us only remember the Studio 28, opened in 1925, where the first projections of *Napoléon* by Abel Gance and *Chien Andalou* by Luis Bunuel took place. There was finally, the largest movie house in Paris, perhaps the largest in all of France, that of the *Gaumont Palace*, just below the cemetery of Montmartre. It was regrettably replace by an apartment building, resting heavily on top of a shopping center.

It is by the cemetery that one day, in May, 1871, a young Communard worker, Jean-Baptiste, gun in hand, left the hill with the hope of fighting elsewhere. The young woman who accompanied him was killed during their escace. It was for her that he wrote, to the music of Renard, *Le Temps des Cerises* (Cherry Time), the refrain of which is still heard in the streets of Paris:

I will always love cherry time, it is then that I have an open wound.

"I understand why Parisians never travel", an English friend of Léon-Paul Fargue explained to him one day. "It is because you have Montmartre! The whole world travels here to see it. You only have to climb up there."

It is true that this climb is a trip through a village where ghosts hover along-side curious visitors, merrymakers, night-owls and quiet residents, indifferent to the din thrown off by the big city. They jealously guard the secret charm of their houses and hidden gardens.

The Eiffel Tower

In order to celebrate the centennial of the French Revolution and the Human Rights Declaration, a new Universal Exhibition was held in Paris in 1889. The Organization Committee decided to create an exceptional monument, a huge iron tower. The Americans had wanted to achieve this same goal for the Philadelphia Exhibition, but hadn't succeeded. The tower was to be one thousand feet tall (300 metres), and have a square base, each side measuring over four hundred and ten feet (125 metres).

A contest was launched on the first of May, 1886, but the brief time allowed the contestants was hotly criticized.

"A contest has been opened. Within fifteen days, between the third and the eighteenth of May, architects or engineers will have to come up with this fantastic tower, a poor sister to the Tower of Babel."

Out of more than 700 entries, that of Gustave Eiffel was chosen. His enormous experience and the fact that he had already realized metal constructions all over Europe (bridges, viaducts), acted strongly in his favor.

The work site captured and held the attention of the Parisians for two years. In *The Paris Pedestrian*, Léon-Paul Fargue recounts: "I watched the Eiffel Tower growing. As we students came out of school, we'd go over to see it. Holding our breath, we could distinguish a red haze of work in progress above the first platform. There was a vague buzz of sound, and we could hear from time to time the pounding of a hammer, like the beat of wings of a raven falling to the dust. A passing official stopped close by us. He was red-faced and blowing, puffed out like a pot-bellied stove with a small officer's collar and his glasses resting on his moustache. He had a watch chain as big as a pair of handcuffs and an inverted inkwell on his head. 'We will never be ready', he declared."

Fargue's official was wrong. The tower was completed by March, 1889.

The tower, which symbolizes the technical capacities of a whole period in the art of metal construction and the flawless mastery of its creator, Gustave Eiffel, as well as that of the entire French industry, was attacked even before it had seen the light of day. Its detractors styled themselves *Ardent lovers of beauty*. In February, 1887, they wrote a petition addressed to M. Alphand, General Direction of the Exhibition Construction: "We come, writers, painters, sculptors, architects; ardent lovers of the beauty of Paris, to protest with all our force and all our indignation, in the name of degraded French taste; in the name of art and threatened French history, against the erection, in the very heart of our capital, of the useless and monstrous Eiffel Tower. Because the Eiffel Tower, which even commercial America

would not want, is doubtless a dishonor to Paris! When foreigners come to visit our Exhibition, they will be surprised. 'What?' they will cry, 'Is this the horror that the French have found, to give us an idea of their so-prized taste?' They would be right to laugh at us if the Paris of gothic splendors, the Paris of Jean Goujon, of Germain Pilon, of Puget, of Rude, of Barye, etc. were to become the Paris of M. Eiffel."

This letter was signed by Maupassant, Alexandre Dumas, Leconte de Lisle, Sully-Prudhomme, Charles Garnier, the painter Meissonier; and even by the composer Charles Gounod, who quickly changed his mind to the point of composing a *Concerto in the Clouds*, which was played on the evening of the inauguration of the Tower, on September 11, 1889.

Others were ironical about the practicalities of its construction and wondered, "Can there be aerial workers as there are underground workers, or miners? Shall we see, next to the mole laborer, a bird laborer?"

When it was finished, the poet Paul Verlaine admitted he would make special detours to avoid having to see it!

Today, over a thousand feet tall (320 metres), including a TV aerial on its top, flanked by one thousand six hundred and fifty-two steps, with iron weighing nine thousand tons; the Eiffel Tower soon came to embody the nineteenth century idea of modernity.

"Everything I like on the other side of the Atlantic I find here", exclaimed Jean Giraudoux. As for the poet Apollinaire, he cast it in the role of debonaire guardian angel: "Shepherdess, O Eiffel Tower, the herd of bridges is bleating this morning..." It would inspire painters like Delaunay, Dufy, Chagall, Utrillo, Fernand Léger and Rousseau. That which had been built for only twenty years is today, although a hundred years old, the symbol of Paris and its most famous monument. Its slender height inimitably dominates the capital city. As Blaise Cendrars put it: "At the end of the field the Eiffel Tower, poised on tiptoe, bends over the roofs and dives into the streets."

From 1916 on, the Tower became an essential communication center. At the beginning it was used for trans-oceanic wireless communication. Then in 1918 a radio broadcasting antenna was installed. Since 1957 French Television has put up its antenna, adding just under 65 feet (20 metres) to its height. The view alone that it affords is enough to justify the Tower's existence. On the first level, a museum tells the story of the Tower's most glorious moments. The second level houses the highest restaurant in Paris: The *Jules Verne* combines the pleasures of superb gastronomy with an unforgettable view. At night the city lights form starry patterns and the illuminated city monuments are transformed into constellations.

Finally, on the topmost level, in fair weather one can see a panorama as far as over forty-three miles (70 kilometres) round. It was here that Eiffel kept an "apartment" for himself.

In 1989, to celebrate the Tower's hundredth birthday, the city of Paris installed a new system of illumination that makes it more than ever the nocturnal shepherdess of Paris. At its feet a figure of Gustave Eiffel, sculpted by Boudelle, keeps watch.

In order to protect it from rust and erosion, the Tower has to be repainted every seven years. Each time a minimum of twenty thousand tons of paint is necessary. Then three shades of brown are applied. The darkest shade goes on the base, working up to the lightest shade at the summit so as to bring out the illusion of lightness fleeing upward to the sky.

The Trocadéro

Opposite the Eiffel Tower, on the right bank of the Seine, rises the hill of Trocadéro with the Chaillot palace. This complex, consisting of two great wings separated by a vast esplanade, was constructed for the Universal Exhibition of 1937. It houses the Museum of Man, the Naval Museum and the Museum of French Monuments. The latter came into being because of an idea of Viollet-le-Duc, who restored some of the greatest of the French monuments, i.e. the medieval site of Carcassone, today a thriving town and a mecca for tourists. The museum contains over two thousand castings and reproductions of the most remarkable architectural elements of the country. In one of the wings, in 1951, the Théâtre National Populaire was installed, created by Jean Vilar. Though it no longer exists today, the TNP is considered the greatest theatrical venture of Paris and France since the Second World War. Gérard Philipe, Maria Casarès and Vilar were the principal players, but many other great names of the theatre were discovered here, such as Sylvia Monfort, Philippe Noiret, Jean Darras, etc.

The splendid terrace of the Trocadéro is one of the favorite gathering places for Parisians and tourists alike. From it one can look down on descending gardens and vast lawns scattered with statues, pools, an old-style merry-go-round and an aquarium, flanked by two symmetrical walks and fountains in a direct line to the Eiffel Tower, it forms a connecting link between the Tower and the hill which faces it.

Les Halles and Saint-Eustache

There is almost nothing left of what was once the central market of Paris. The quarter of Les Halles was, for several centuries, the heart and stomach of the city. This bustling market was transferred outside Paris to the suburb of Rungis in 1970, and since then all agree that the once lively quarter has lost its soul. In place of the market stands the Forum des Halles, a commercial center inaugured in 1976. This modern development will never make the picturesque world of the former market live again, the same world that Zola and other writers wrote about in glorious prose and poetry.

Forgotten are the women of Les Halles, who treasured the priviledge, from Louis XIV onwards, of being allowed to insult the king. Forgotten are the Forts des Halles, the butchers who had to do heavy carrying, and who kept themselves going by swearing and gulping coarse red wine. Forgotten are the women who ladled out soup, who peeled vegetables, the men who measured and counted out eggs, who poured out the fish. Forgotten are the cries of the fish auctioners and the many and varied calls of the itinerant vendors in the Carreau des Halles.

On the eve of the French Revolution the local inhabitants were granted their wish that the old charnal house with its gruesome odors be replaced by the Marché des Innocents. Today all that remains of the old market is the fountain of Jean Goujon which borders the cheap clothes market. In the Rue Saint-Denis they now chase away the prostitutes whose charms have been sung by poets from Villon to Breton, to protect "in vogue" shop windows and the over-polished sidewalks. Mediocre stores which claim to be "à la mode" have replaced one of the old smoking rooms where Desnos and Aragon sat dreaming by the coffee percolators. The Rue Rambuteau in no longer covered by those graceful structures of iron and glass that Balterd built during the 1860's ten superb pavilions that were bitterly regretted almost as soon as they were demolished. President Pompidou upon whom the architectural past of Paris seems to have made no impression, pushed ahead their destruction. Confronted with those people who denounced a massacre, he became ironic.

"After all, it's not really the Parthenon!" Perhaps! But what about the wretched gardens and the Forum which have taken their place; an afflictive image of the type of urban planning that tries to innovate and is merely futile.

The one remaining vestal of the past is the church of Saint-Eustache. Its construction, begun in 1532, went on for over a century. It combines the Gothic style with that of the Renaissance. Richelieu, Molière and Madame de Pompadour were christened there. Louis XIV had his first communion there; Rameau is buried there, along with La Fontaine and Molière. As Molière was an actor, he was at first refused Christian burial. Louis XIV had to intervene personally with the Archbishop of Paris before he could be buried there after a religious service... by night!

Saint-Eustache is also one of the high spots of Parisian musical life. It was here that Berlioz gave the first performance of his *Te Deum*; here Liszt played his *Mess de Gran*. Today there is still an organ festival every year.

The Pompidou Center

From Les Halles along the Rue Rambuteau, we cross the Rue Quincampoix and discover Beaubourg.

The plateau of Beaubourg was for a long time one of the most insalubrious and filthy quarters of Paris. In its ancient narrow streets, the XVIIth and XVIIIth century buildings remained standing only thanks to strong wooden props. Part of the plateau had become, during the 1960's, a vast vacant lot which, during the day, served as a free parking lot. It was here that President Georges Pompidou decided to create a center for contemporary art. He wanted it to be "a grand architectural gesture". The monument astonished more than one person. Its vivid colors, its protruding structures, its walls of glass and metal tubes inspired more mockery than praise. Parisians were not slow to give it lively nicknames: "The Refinery", "The Giant Mecano (Tinker Toy)", "The Culture Steamer", "The Pompidoleum", etc. Renamed with the name of the man who had thought it up, the Center of Art and Culture Georges Pompidou is today one of the most visited sights of Paris, as much by Parisians as by tourists! An average of twenty-five thousand visitors a day crowds through its portals. And this success has not stopped since the first day it opened, on January 31, 1977.

The concentration of everything concerning contemporary creation into one place has been and is, more than its architecture, the essential reason for this popular success. Indeed, throughout its hundred thousand square meters of surface distributed over eight floors, three of which are below ground level, the Art and Culture center is full of interesting material. In addition to temporary shows of major importance, there is the National Museum of Modern Art. This contains some very rich collections illustrative of the period between 1905 and 1965. There is a constant renewal and presentation of currant art, rooms dedicated to the photography department and a very large public library. A vast and complete center of contemporary music is also to be found here, and, from the upper terraces, a splendid panoramic view. The surroundings are sadly not up to the ambitious level of renewal that has upset them. The garish façades of the buildings that ring the immense square that fronts the Center have already lost whatever charm they might have once had. In the Quartier de l'Horloge (the great Clock), alone amidst a group of lackluster buildings, only the Clock itself attracts clusters of tourists every hour on the hour. Otherwise the *Passage de l'Horloge*, once the shops have closed, is almost desolate.

The reverse is the case of the Place Igor Stravinsky, which lies between the main square and the Rue Saint-Merri. The pool and fountain, created by Tinguely and Niky de Saint-Phalle, represent various works by the composer of the *Firebird* with impish charm and humour.

The Hôtel de Ville

It was in 1260 that Louis IX founded the municipality of Paris. The responsability for it was put in the hands of the Prévôt, the titular head of the merchants and aldermen. By this gesture, the King gave the City certain rights as far as the police, commerce, navigation and city organization were concerned. These rights, however, were subject to and limited by royal power.

The seat of the municipality was originally installed in the Place du Châtelet, on the Ile de la Cité. The City Provost was Etienne Marcel, whose statue is still standing in the City Hall gardens, its original setting. It had earlier been transferred in 1357 to the Maison aux Piliers on the Place de Grève, today called the Place de l'Hôtel de Ville (the site of today's City Hall). The Place de Grève was for a long time a place where the jobless could come together, hoping to find work. From this practice the expression evolved to "Faire la Grève" means to go on strike, a similarity with a difference!

In 1533 the Maison aux Piliers collapsed, and François I ordered a new edifice built on the site. The replacement was constantly altered and enlarged. It was concerned in and with all the great happenings in France up to 1871, when it was burnt by the Communards. The Third Republic decided to reconstruct it, taking its inspiration from the defunct edifice. The result was the Hôtel de Ville, or City Hall that we see today. The façade is in the neo-Renaissance style, and the interior is a real museum of stuffy art. The rooms are temples to good Republican ideals, illustrated by frescoes and paintings. The Family, the Homeland, Science, Democracy and the People are here sung with fervor under bulging ceilings, loaded with gilded stucco.

Originally this square was the Gallo-Roman port of the Grève. It rapidly became one of the principal places of city activity. The first Paris market, outside the Cité, set up its booths there, up to the XIIth century. Then it became the place of execution for capital crimes. In the Middle Ages, common law criminals were punished by hanging or decapitation, whereas quartering was reserved for offenders of lèse-majesté. It was here, in 1610, that Ravaillac was drawn and quartered. During the French Revolution, the guillotine was installed here for a time.

Not merely a great part of the history of Paris, but also of French history is recorded here on the square and within the walls of the City Hall. There was the time when Etienne Marcel, from his strong hold in the Maison aux Piliers, attempted to arouse the Kingdom against King Charles V. Then came the insurrection of August, 1792, the advent of Louis-Philippe and the adoption of the tricolor flag in 1830, the proclamation of the Second Republic in 1848 and that of the Commune in 1871. Not to forget the Liberation of Paris in 1944. In 1977, Paris took to itself a Mayor who administered twenty Deputy Mayors, one for each of the twenty arrondissements of the city. The City Hall then also became the Mayor's residence.

The Marais

Behind the City Hall, along the Rue de Rivoli and extending along the Rue Saint-Antoine as far as the Bastille, lies the Marais. This ancient and former quagmire, covered with mud every time the Seine overflowed, is where one of the most aristocratic quarters of Paris was erected.

"Before it became a veritable museum of ancient 'hôtels' and palaces, all rivalling each other in elegance and superb taste... the Marais was, quite simply, a marsh (a marais). (...) This part of Paris was covered with rushes, long-stemmed weeds, willows and wormwood. A strong odor of mint warred with the perfumed hair powder of the aristocratic ladies of the XVIIth-century..." Léon-Paul Fargue tells us.

This marshland was cut through by two old Roman roads leading to, respectively, the East and Senlis. They eventually became the Rue Saint-Antoine and the Rue Saint-Martin.

By the end of the XIIth century there were four neighbouring quarters, protected by the enclosing walls built by Philippe-Auguste and huddled next to their churches: Saint-Germain-l'Auxerrois, les Halles, la Grève and Saint-Gervais. The terrain situated to the north and outside the walls was still a swamp. Starting from the Rue Saint-Antoine were to grow lanes that today are the Rue Saint-Paul, the Rue du Roi de Sicile, the Rue Vieille-du-Temple and the Rue du Temple. These latter were named after the Knights Templar who were the first, from the end of the XIIIthcentury, to take over the land and set up a new city, complete with a street system and shops.

King Charles V, in the XIVth century, gave the Marais a decided lift when he quit his palace on the Ile de la Cité and moved into the hôtel Saint-Pol, between the Seine and the Rue Saint-Antoine. His family followed him, along with a number of great nobles. In 1528

François I in turn moved in and parcelled off the magnificent quarter of the Rue des Francs-Bourgeois. Here would be erected some of the most beautiful mansions of the Marais, including the Carnavalet, today a fascinating museum.

The growth of the Marais was cut short by the religious wars, until Henri IV commisioned Sully to erect a place that would rapidly become a favored meeting place of the aristocracy and of Parisian finance: the Place Royale, today known as the Place des Vosges. The last fields which were left were then parcelled off. During the Grand Siècle, or Great Century, in the reign of Louis XIV, everything that counted for anything in Paris went through the Marais: the great state officials and the greatest financiers, like Aubert de Fontenay. He was a former lackey grown rich who was responsible for having the Hôtel Salé built. Then there were magistrates such as Lamoignon, whose "hôtel", Rue Pavée, today holds the Bibliothèque Historique de la Ville de Paris. There were writers, one of whom was Madame de Sévigné, who lived in the hôtel Carnavalet. The XVIIth century was the Marais' golden century. But the splendid hôtels of Soubise and de Rohan were the last princely dwellings. Little by little the Marais was supplanted in the hearts of the Parisian aristocracy by the Faubourg Saint-Germain and the Faubourg Saint-Honoré.

The Marais was the first quarter to be touched by the French Revolution. The taking of the Bastille followed by its destruction removed what had long been a bastion of protection. The quarter emptied, the dwellings of aristocrats who had emigrated were taken over and sequestrated as of 1792. The XIXth century saw the installation of schools in the old hôtels of Carnavalet, of Mayenne, of Beauvais or of Marle, as well as in the Cloître (Cloister) des Minimes. Artists, in particular writers, continued to live there. Victor Hugo of course, whose house on the Place des Vosges has been made into a museum. But Balzac and Théophile Gautier lived there as well. Flaubert lived in the Rue du Temple; Alphonse Daudet and then his son, Léon, occupied the hôtel of Lamoignon. The whole of the literary world met regularly in the Arsenal library, whose head was Charles Nodier. But in the last half of the XIXth century, it is particularly the advent of the industrial revolution that strikes the imagination. Daudet evokes this time in his *Paris vécu*: "To the rear of our Hôtel Lamoignon there was a chemical factory. They were all over the Marais, along with wholesale pharmaceutical product firms. Children's toys, chemical and pharmaceutical products, haberdashery and notions traders, woolstuffs and warehouses, wholesale jewelers and pawnbrokers, spare parts, bars and bronze statues, dental clinics and carpenter shops filled, from top to bottom, all these former stately dwellings."

On another plane, Giraudoux considers that "this sanctifying occupation of the quarter by small businesses and craftsmen was what saved the Marais from the wholesale transformation carried out all over Paris by Haussmann". Certainly the destruction of so many hôtels did not begin till the time of the Third Republic. Then, for example, they tore down the hôtel d'Effiat to open up the Rue du Trésor; the Cloître des Minimes was razed to make way for a military barracks; the magnificent Hôtel de la Vieuville disappeared and in its place they built warehouses for the department store, La Samaritaine.

The last one to disappear was the Hôtel de la Michaudière, in the Rue des Archives, in 1969. This was in spite of a new law put through by Michel Debré and André Malraux creating protected sectors, like the Marais! Since this law, strengthend by a plan of safeguard and developed in 1992, the Marais has come back to life. We can hope that the hôtels and their façades, witnesses to so many centuries, will be forever preserved and kept up. You can walk around the tiny streets in the quarter and push open doors that can hide treasures: sleeping parks, paved courts and dwellings forgotten by time.

One of the easiest to visit is at number 5, Rue Thorigny. This hôtel was turned into a museum in 1985, and it contains the Picasso collection. It was constructed between 1656 and 1658 for Pierre Aubert de Fontenay, a former lackey. He became a "farmer of Gabelles", that is he collected the taxes levied on salt. The hôtel takes its name from its former owner's activity; the hôtel Salé. The hôtel has had numerous tenants, notably, in chronological order: the Venetian Ambassador, at the end of the XVIIth century; Madame de Sévigné; Maréchal Villeroy, who was Governer under Louis XV; the Ecole Centrale, from 1829 to 1884; the family of artists in bronze-casting, Vian, who were the last tenants before the hôtel became a museum. One of the children of that family was Boris Vian, the writer of many talents. The hôtel was in very poor condition when the City of Paris took it over in 1962. It was carefully restored from 1978 to 1985, when it became the Picasso Museum. To the superb stone and stucco decorations was added the elegance of chandeliers, lanterns and torches designed by Diego Giacometti. The great Spanish master (Picasso) is here revealed in all his wealth of creativity: paintings (for example *Les Demoiselles d'Avignon*), sculptures, collages, ceramiques, drawings, engravings... Picasso's personal collection of paintings is present as well, with canvases by Cézanne, Renoir, Matisse, Miro, Braque, Juan Gris, etc.

It would take some time to enumerate all the hôtels in the Marais that can still be admired. To take a few examples: in the Rue des Archives is the house of Jacques Cœur, at number 40; at number 60 in the same street, the Musée de la Chasse et de la Nature (the Hunt and Nature Museum),

an admirable work by Mansart. In the Rue du Temple the hôtels Saint-Aignan and Montmor are neighbours. In the latter, in 1666, the first experiment in the transfusion of human blood took place, and Molière came here to read *Tartuffe*, when his play was banned. Located at number 60 in the Rue des Franc-Bourgeois is the Hôtel Soubise, one of the chefs-d'œuvre of the quarter which has been the repository of the national archives since 1808. It contains a remarkable museum of the history of France. At 87 Rue Vieille du Temple is the Hôtel de Rohan, which has also had national archives assigned to it, but only since 1938. Up to then the important work of restoration of the papers was being completed. They were in a practically moribund state, left by the national printers and their typographers.

On the corner of the Rue de Sévigné and the Rue des Francs-Bourgeois lies one of the jewels of Renaissance architecture in Paris: the Musée Carnavalet. Erected in 1545, it was acquired in 1580 by Madame de Kernevoy, the widow of a Breton aristocrat. It was the deformation of this name that turned it into Carnavalet. After Mansart, in 1655, had given the building its present appearance, the Marquise de Sévigné lived there for twenty years. The City of Paris took it over in 1866, and it became a museum whose collections are exclusively devoted to the history of Paris. We cannot finish this walk through the Marais without evoking the Hôtel de Sully, perhaps the most beautiful of all. Situated between the Rue Saint-Antoine and the Place des Vosges and constructed in 1624, it became six years later the property of a former Minister of Henry IV, Maximilien de Béthune, Duke of Sully, who gave it its name. Its court of honor, which gives onto the Rue Saint-Antoine; its façades; its French-style garden, and the Orangerie, whose walls are the same walls as the Place des Vosges; all these factors together make the Hôtel de Sully an exceptional ensemble of elements of

Louis XIII architecture. One December evening in 1725, as he was leaving the hôtel where he had been the guest of the fifth Duke of Sully, Voltaire was badly and vigorously thrashed by the servants of the Chevalier de Rohan-Chabot, in the Rue Saint-Antoine. Rohan-Chabot had been cut to the quick by the biting wit the poet had used at his expense.

"Don't hit me too hard on the head!" cried Voltaire. "Something good might still come out of it!" As he had no intention of letting matters stand, Voltaire wanted to challenge the Chevalier to a duel... he was subsequently sent to the Bastille, where he remained for a month. At the far end of the Hôtel de Sully garden on the left of the Orangerie, a tall gate opens onto the place des Vosges.

The Place des Vosges

Fargue tells us, "The chef-d'œuvre of the Marais with its hundred hôtels, with its thousand little tangled streets, (...) the masterpiece of this Paris which is so complete, is the Place Royale, today named Place des Vosges. This in honor of the first French department (county) which paid its contributions in full in the year VIII..."

This square, constructed between 1605 and 1612, covers the site of the former royal residence of Charles V, the Hôtel des Tournelles and a part of its gardens.

The Place des Vosges was inaugurated in 1612, to celebrate the engagement of Louis XIII and the infanta of Spain.

In 1739, at Richelieu's initiative, a statue of Louis XIII was erected in the center of the square. Then a garden was put in... but a garden without trees so as not to cover up the lovely order of façades of the thirty houses. In the early morning duels were fought, and when evening fell the arcades lent themselves to games of courtship and gallantry.

It was only in 1783, at the request of the inhabitants, that trees were planted. During the Revolution the statue of Louis XIII was, like so many others in Paris, knocked down. It wasn't replaced until 1829 by the present statue, which shows the king as a Roman emperor.

Today the square has rediscovered a bit of its former luster. Most of the hôtels have been restored. Under the arcades, resturants and picture galleries attract strollers. Once again, as they did in the Grand Siècle, celebrities and prominent people make their homes there. Politics and the arts are neighbours.

At number 6, the house where Victor Hugo lived for sixteen years, is a museum with a considerable amount of mementoes and souvenirs of the writer.

Close to the Place des Vosges and enclosed between the Rue de Rivoli, the Rue Pavée, the Rue des Archives and the Rue des Francs-Bourgeois, lies the *Pletzl*, the Jewish quarter of the Marais. Since the Jewish people first settled in Paris more than two thousand years ago, they have suffered constant persecution, banishment and expulsion in and from the city. Even the King of France himself, the "good" Saint Louis, didn't he go so far as to make it mandatory for Jews to pin a little yellow wheel on their chests? This was so that people could know who were the useful moneylenders, but who were held in contempt by the rest of the population.

Jews were initially installed on the islands (they came with the Romans to Lutèce, as Paris was called then, and later put up a synagogue on the Ile de la Cité on the site of what is now the hospital of the Hôtel-Dieu). They were in the Latin Quarter during the XIIth century when Philippe-Auguste, who had driven them out of the Cité in 1182, recalled them twelve years later. Massive expulsions redoubled during the XVth century, and Paris was practically emptied of its Jewish community. But when the Eastern European pogroms drove them westward at the beginning of the XIXth century, they returned to Paris to settle in the heart of the Marais around the Rue des Rosiers. Kosher grocers, restaurants and specialized bookshops are to be found there. In the Rue Pavée stands the superb façade of the synagogue, built in 1913 by one of the most famous Art Nouveau French architects, Hector Guimard. The metal structure is by Gustave Eiffel.

The Bastille

For a long time the Marais lived under the protection of the Bastille. Built in 1370 by Charles V, the Bastille was originally a fortified castle, a veritable military fortress to protect both the Porte Saint-Antoine and the Hôtel Saint-Pol, where the King resided. As of 1382, Charles VI, who completed it, used it as a prison for "wrong thinkers". Writers who stepped beyond the accepted lines, stubborn Protestants and libertines were sent there, generally for shortish stays. This continued for six centuries. Among the more notable prisoners we can find Voltaire, the Marquis de Sade or a young man named Latude. Otherwise obscure, he became famous by frightening the Marquise de Pompadour. He informed her of a plot against her, but the plot was false.

As time went on, the Bastille became a symbol of an arbitrary and absolute monarchy. There were plans to demolish it well before 1789, agreed to by Louis XVI. Sébastien Mercier wrote in 1788: "The fortress that Charles V had built is still standing, despite the fact that we have already razed it on paper. But it must come down one of these days. When am I going to see an equestrian statue in place of the Bastille?"

By 1783 Linguet had proposed putting a statue of Louis XIV as replacement of the prison.

Necker, the Finance Minister who found the upkeep of the prison too expensive, planned on demolishing seven of the eight towers. A statue of the King was to be placed on the top of the remaining tower.

In 1784, the architect Courbet drew up plans for *Une place publique à la gloire de Louis XVI*, a sort of new Place Royale. This would be in eastern Paris, and meanwhile there would be the Place Louis XV, which is now the Place de la Concorde.

But the fourteenth of July, 1789, brought all these plans to nothing and precipitated the demolition of the prison, which became a mythical image of Revolutionary History.

Héron de Villefosse tells the story: "At the Bastille, Governor Launay was in command of thirty Swiss and eighty-two disabled men. He had blocked the crenellations and raised the draw-bridge. Some shots were fired while they were parleying. When he perceived some uniforms of the French guardsmen, he surrendered unconditionally. He was cut to pieces by the cook, Desnot. The victors didn't yet dream that their wretched combat would go down in history as the most glorious day in the History of France. They went from room to room, (the eight dungeons had been empty for fifteen years), and delivered the prisoners.

"The Paris populace freed and gave back their liberty, on the fourteenth of July, 1789, to four forgers who should have been in the Châtelet, to two madmen who rightly belonged in Charenton and the Comte de Solages, a dissolute young man whose family paid the administration a pension of two thousand eight hundred pounds to keep him...

"The prisoners of the Bastille for two centuries had frequently been guests, as was Voltaire, at the Governor's dinner table, where they dined on game and shellfish, washed down with champagne

130

and burgundy. Many newspapers were allowed in to the prisoners.

"Once this high luxury prison had fallen, it was imperative to make the most of this easy victory and rale against the old towers, witnesses of an odious past."

The poet André Chenier, in singing about it, helped boost the idea of a horrid prison before he died on the scaffold, destroyed like the Bastille by a certain idea of Liberty which was not shared by all the revolutionaries.

The hell of the Bastille, to all winds thrown
Fly, infamous remains and inanimate ashes
And from these great tombs, beautiful Liberty
Haughty, shining, armed
Emerges...

It was Napoléon's idea to place an elephant with a tower on its back on the ruins of the Bastille. Only the plaster model was prepared and placed, but it didn't hold out long against the weather. Victor Hugo described it in *Les Misérables*: "It was a sort of symbol of the popular forces. it was dark, enigmatic and immense. It was who-knows-what powerful ghost, visible and upright next to the invisible specter of the Bastille."

Since 1831 the Spirit of Liberty has dominated the place de la Bastille from the top of its 154 foot (47 metres) column of July. It never ceases to fly and flourish the torch of Liberty, breaking the chains of servitude. (A replica of this statue by the sculptor Dumont is on view at the Louvre in the Richelieu wing.)

This column was erected to celebrate the revolution of 1830 and the three glorious, great days when the people of Paris overthrew the monarchy of Charles X, the brother of Louis XVI, to replace it by... that of Louis-Philippe, the nephew of Louis XVI!

The pedestal of the column is none other than the pedestal that supported the plaster model of Napoléon's elephant. In 1854 the Louvre moats were cleared out. Here were also the bodies of the July, 1830, fighting which had been hastily shoveled under the day after the battle in the streets. They had joined some forgotten Egyptian mummies which no doubt had been considered "unworthy" to enter the Museum. They were all taken and buried under the column along with the victims of the 1848 revolution. It is thus that, in the Place de la Bastille, no-one stops to contemplate or meditate and honor the dead of two of last century's revolutions.

Since 1989 there is a new monument standing in the place de la Bastille: the Opéra Bastille. Inaugurated on the fourteenth of July, 1989, this modern opera house was constructed on the site of the symbolic prison.

It took five years to build. The Canadian architect, Carlos Ott, who designed it, directed its construction. This immense geometric pile covers an area of a hundred and fifty thousand square metres; it is forty-eight metres high. A futuristic temple to grand opera, it offers performing artists the best technical and acoustical conditions. The glacial immoderacy of its vast halls, the endless connecting passages whose cold starkness confined to emptiness, are hardly conducive to lyric festivities. However the great auditorium, with its two thousand seven hundred seats, is the largest opera house in France. With unceasing strikes and various conflicts and seat prices often judged prohibitive, this opera house, supposedly for the people, has been so far a stronghold more difficult of assault than was the prison of the same name.

Captions for photographs
73 to 94

73. *The Forum des Halles, inaugurated in 1976, and the church of Saint-Eustache, built from 1519 to 1640.*

74. *The Georges Pompidou Centre for Contemporary Art.*

75. *Near the Pompidou Centre, aquatic sculptures by Nicky de Saint-Palle and Tinguely.*

76. *The Forum des Halles.*

77. *The Fontaine des Innocents (1549) is the oldest fountain in Paris. It is the work of the sculptors Jean Goujon and Pierre Lescot.*

78. *A sphinx from the fountain in the Place du Châtelet. In the distance, the Saint-Jacques tower (1522), fifty-two meters high.*

79. *The front of the Hôtel de Ville. The building was entirely rebuilt in 1873, after having been burned during the Paris Commune.*

80. *The Arsenal canal and the Place de la Bastille, with the July (1832) column and the Bastille-Opéra (1989).*

81. *The Bastille Opéra at night.*

82. *The génie of the Bastille atop the July Column. This monument, erected in honor of the revolution of 1830, prompted Victor Hugo to write: It is the would-be monument to a failed revolution.*

83. *The Place des Vosges. Built by Henri IV, it was inaugurated in 1612, two years after his death, to celebrate Louis XIII's engagement to the infanta of Spain.*

84. *The grand staircase of the Hôtel Salé (1656). This building in the Marais is a museum today and houses the works and personal collections of Picasso.*

85. *The Orangerie of the Hôtel Sully (1625-1630). The door in the pavilion on the right opens directly onto the Place des Vosges.*

86. *The Hôtel de Soubise (1705). This superb building in the Marais is where the National Archives are kept.*

87. *The Hôtel de Sens, in the Saint-Paul quarter, houses the Forney Library.*

88. *The pullring on a mansion door in the Marais.*

89. *The Saint-Martin canal and the Tournant bridge. This canal was dug under the Restauration, during the 1820's, to link the Seine with the Ourcq canal.*

90. *The Temple of Love (le temple d'Amour) in the Buttes-Chaumont park, one of the many parks created under Napoléon III (1867).*

91. *Resting on the lawn. Which park is this? Monceau, Montsouris, the Bois de Boulogne or the Bois de Vincennes? So many parks were created or re-designed by Alphand under the Second Empire.*

92. *Rowing on the artificial lake in the Buttes-Chaumont park.*

93. *The Cité de la Villette.*

94. *One of the numerous Morris fountains offered to the city of Paris at the end of the XIXth century by the American patron of art, whose name they bear.*

74

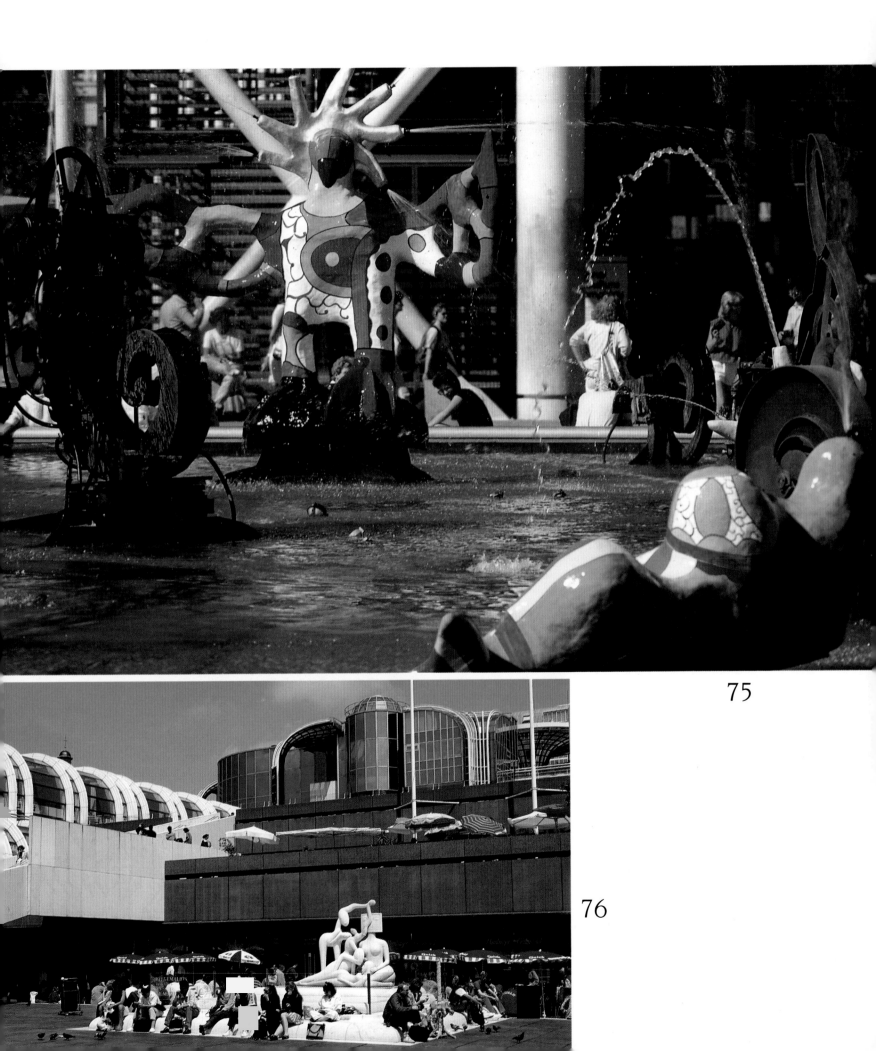

75

76

77

78

81

94

Since the nineteen eighties Paris has been preparing for the XXIst century. What have been called the Grands Travaux (Great Works) are typical of this will for modernity and adaptation. The festivities for the Bicentennial of the French Revolution spawned, with great Republican pomp: The inauguration of the Grande Arche of La Défense, the Finance Ministry in Bercy, the Cité of Science and Industry at La Villette, the Pyramide of the Grand Louvre, the Opéra Bastille and the Musée d'Orsay. President Mitterrand, like all powerful men in this world since antiquity, has inscribed thus his claims to eternity. Monuments are more certain to assure the perennial memory of "great men" than their policies.

But the Grands Travaux are also interesting in that they reveal what our ideas are about the next century. This is exemplified by the Grande Arche of La Défense, the Finance Ministry and the Grande Bibliothèque (Great Library), which is soon to open. All combine ultra-modern techniques with barren aesthetic values. The straightness and the enormous size of the façades reveal the icy ambition of these buildings: harshness, rationality, efficiency and modernity are the master designers of this symbolic architecture of our time. One could go so far as to say that the buildings are "intelligent"!

According to our architects and city planners, the twenty-first century will be the age of efficiency and aesthetic purification. At least that's what they think. But sometimes stripped-down elegance can be sterile chill.

Only the Grand Louvre and the Musée d'Orsay escape this systematic nudity.

The early architecture of their façades and the live warmth of the works of art within them are the reason for this.

Let up hope that many artists will continue to see Paris as their capital. May their souls temper the harshness of those in charge of what it is to become. May they both, artists and planners, live and work together in a creative spirit that laughs at rules and the necessary economic efficiency for all modern cities.

Patrice de Moncan

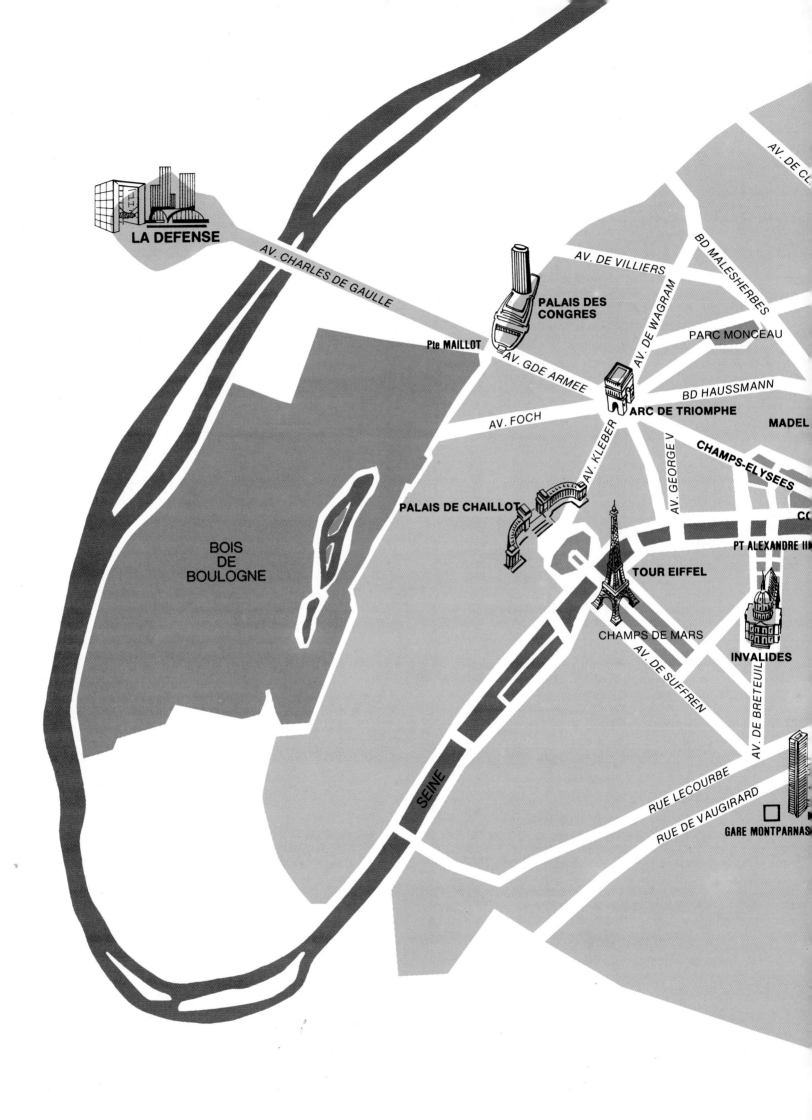

LA DEFENSE

AV. CHARLES DE GAULLE

AV. DE VILLIERS

BD MALESHERBES

PALAIS DES CONGRES

AV. DE WAGRAM

PARC MONCEAU

Pte **MAILLOT**

AV. GDE ARMEE

BD HAUSSMANN

AV. FOCH

ARC DE TRIOMPHE

AV. KLEBER

AV. GEORGE V

MADEL

CHAMPS-ELYSEES

PALAIS DE CHAILLOT

CO

BOIS
DE
BOULOGNE

PT ALEXANDRE III

TOUR EIFFEL

INVALIDES

CHAMPS DE MARS

AV. DE SUFFREN

AV. DE BRETEUIL

SEINE

RUE LECOURBE

RUE DE VAUGIRARD

GARE MONTPARNAS

AV. DE ST OUEN

CIMETIERE
ONTMARTRE

SACRE-CŒUR

PIGALLE

BD BARBES

CLICHY

BD DE CLICHY

LA VILLETTE

AV. JEAN JAURES

BUTTES CHAUMONT

AZARE

RUE LA FAYETTE

GARE DU NORD

BD DE MAGENTA

GARE DE L'EST

OPERA

GRANDS BOULEVARDS

AV. DE L'OPERA

PL. DE LA REPUBLIQUE

PALAIS ROYAL

FORUM
DES HALLES

BD SEBASTOPOL

PL. VENDOME

CENTRE POMPIDOU

CIMETIERE
DU PERE LACHAISE

JARDIN
S TUILERIES

CARROUSEL

TOUR ST-
JACQUES

PLACE DES VOSGES

OPÉRA

PT DES
ARTS

LOUVRE

MAIN-
PRES

PT-NEUF
ILE DE
LA CITE

LE MARAIS

HOTEL-
DE-VILLE

COLONNE DE JUILLET

NOTRE-DAME

BD SAINT GERMAIN

ILE
ST-LOUIS

BD HENRI IV

LA BASTILLE

RUE DU Fbg ST ANTOINE

PL. DE
LA NATION

COURS DE VINCENNES

PICE

ST-ETIENNE-DU-MONT

BD DIDEROT

BD RASPAIL

BD SAINT MICHEL

PALAIS DU
LUXEMBOURG

PANTHEON

JARDIN
DES PLANTES

GARE DE LYON

MONTPARNASSE

GARE D'AUSTERLITZ

BERCY

NASSE

BD DE PORT ROYAL

BD DE L'HOPITAL

SEINE

METIERE
TPARNASSE

PL. DENFERT-ROCHEREAU

BD SAINT JACQUES

PL. D'ITALIE

BOIS
DE
VINCENNES

AV. DU GENERAL LECLERC

AV. D'ITALIE

PARC
MONTSOURIS